It's a Fine Life
My Story

Jodie Prenger
with Christian Guiltenane

MICHAEL O'MARA BOOKS LIMITED

First published in Great Britain in 2009 by
Michael O'Mara Books Limited
9 Lion Yard
Tremadoc Road
London SW4 7NQ

All pictures courtesy of Jodie Prenger, and reproduced with her kind
permission, excepting: page 4 (*middle* and *bottom*) Leila Amanpour;
page 5 (*all pics*) and page 6 (*top*) © BBC; page 7 (*top*) Gerallt Llewelyn;
page 7 (*bottom*) Rex Features; page 8 (*top right* and *bottom*)
Richard Young/Rex Features.

Every reasonable effort has been made to acknowledge all copyright
holders. Any errors or omissions that may have occurred are
inadvertent, and anyone with any copyright queries is invited to write
to the publishers, so that a full acknowledgement may be included in
subsequent editions of this work.

A CIP catalogue record for this book is available from
the British Library.

Papers used by Michael O'Mara Books Limited are natural,
recyclable products made from wood grown in sustainable forests.
The manufacturing processes conform to the environmental
regulations of the country of origin.

ISBN (hardback): 978-1-84317-351-9
ISBN (paperback): 978-1-84317-382-3

1 3 5 7 9 10 8 6 4 2

Designed and typeset by E-Type

Plate section designed by Ana Bjezancevic

Printed in the UK by CPI William Clowes Beccles NR34 7TL

www.mombooks.com

Contents

Author's Acknowledgements

I want to dedicate this book to Cameron Mackintosh and Andrew Lloyd Webber for making my dreams come true. Thanks to all of their team, and to the cast and crew of *Oliver!* for the support they have given me, and for making me feel like part of the family.

To the people at the BBC, the production staff and crew of *I'd Do Anything* and all the Nancys – it was the most amazing experience I've ever had and I will never forget the best summer of my life. A special thank you to John Barrowman for having belief in me from the start.

John, Inny and Saj, and Angie Dowds: thank you for supporting me during my weight-loss journey. I couldn't have done it without you.

Gavin Barker, Steven and Michelle (my new London family), thanks for everything – you're the best.

I also want to say thank you to my fans, and to Christian: without you, Mr Guiltenane, my story would just be a coffee coaster.

Most of all, I want to dedicate this book to Mum, Dad and Marko: my backbone and the most wonderful family a girl could wish for. Nan and Granddad – thanks for watching over me. Thanks also to Aunty Olga, Aunty Aideen, Simon and Sam; and of course my dogs (even if they can't read this). Thanks to you all for being there every step of the way. This is for you.

Jodie Prenger, 2009

Introduction

It's here. It's really here. Tonight's the chuffin' night that I've been waiting for the whole of my life. After years of struggling and grafting my arse off, my dreams are finally about to come true.

This evening – Wednesday 14 January 2009 – I, Jodie Christine Prenger, will step out on stage a West End star. I will play to a packed house, and for this night in particular, I know that all eyes will be on me. I'm nervous. Hell, that's the understatement of the century. But I can do it. Can't I?

Sitting backstage in my dressing room that evening, counting down the minutes before my final call, before my debut in *Oliver!*'s opening night, my heart was doing a *Riverdance* in my chest. Studying myself in the mirror, I gazed into the eyes of a person I'd never thought I'd become.

I looked pretty calm. Underneath, it was a different story. I was totally bricking it. In fact, I was feeling so frickin' nervous that I thought I could actually do myself a mischief. Taking a deep breath, I managed to keep myself under control – which was a relief not only to myself, but also to my cast mates and those folks who have to clean up after us at the Theatre Royal Drury Lane. Yet there was no getting away from it. I still felt like a bowl of jelly, quivering in my seat.

Now, don't get me wrong: I love performing, I really do. I adore getting up on stage and seeing an audience enjoying itself. It was just that, this time, I knew there was a lot riding on my performance. You see, tonight, Matthew, I was going to be Nancy, the tart with a heart, in Cameron Mackintosh's brand spanking new production of Lionel Bart's classic musical *Oliver!* Yes, can you believe it? Jolly Jodie Prenger from Blackpool was about to become a West End leading lady.

I should have been 100 per cent excited and raring to go; and in some ways I was, like a kid at Christmas. I couldn't wait to get out there. After all, it was what I had been born to do.

Nevertheless, given the circumstances, the pressure I was under was immense. The next two hours were make-or-break: two hours to knock the socks off the toughest crowd I'd ever faced; one hundred and twenty minutes to prove myself to the world.

Once upon a time, I was a roly-poly cabaret singer and part-time agony aunt who wasn't sure what to do with her life. Then, after winning the BBC's *I'd Do Anything*, my world changed beyond recognition.

I was now set to appear in one of the most famous musicals in the world, in London's prestigious West End. Who'd have thought it, eh? My name up in lights. It was a right shock to me, that's for sure. I'd only ever dreamed of starring in the West End, and I knew that dreams like that rarely came true for normal people like me.

Instead, I'd settled for banging out classic numbers at grotty working men's clubs all around the north-west of England. The closest I had ever got to performing to packed houses prior to my Nancy experience was at Alton Towers' *Spooktacular* show, on the Disney cruises off the coast of Florida, and at a Pontin's weekend.

Yet, thanks to the British public, I finally had a chance to make something of myself. At last, I had been given an opportunity to achieve my goals and fulfil my potential – and it was all down to my fans. Comfy at home on their sofas, the British public had watched me singing my heart out and acting my socks off every week on the TV show. They must have seen or heard something they liked, because at the end of the twelve-week run, it was me they chose as their Nancy.

Yes, I won the bloody thing. It was an amazing feeling, let me tell you. And as corny as it sounds, all of a sudden I felt loved and accepted and that anything was possible. That sounds dramatic or like some kind of Hollywood movie, but you have to bear in mind that for much of my life I was busy dragging around a fair bit of extra weight with me – and I'm not talking a few additional pounds; I'm talking 20 frickin' stone.

You got it: I was a porker. I was 'larger than life'. In simple terms, I was a bloater. So, as you can imagine, for years and years I just didn't have the kind of 'look' producers were searching for. My face didn't fit. Come to think of it, neither did my arse.

When I won 'Nancy', as *I'd Do Anything* was commonly known, I was over the bloody moon, but I was scared, too. You see, while it felt incredible to be named as the nation's favourite Nancy, with it came pressure. I realized that I couldn't let down the people who had put me on that stage. The public had chosen me, spent their hard-earned cash voting for me – I owed it to them to be sensational. Anything less, in my mind, would have been like sticking two fingers up at all of them. I needed to be good not just for me, but for the people who had invested so much of their time and money in me. As I sat in my dressing room, I hoped desperately that I wouldn't let my nerves get the better of me.

And it wasn't just the public I needed to impress. Let's not forget Lord Lloyd-Webber and Sir Cameron Mackintosh, the big wigs behind the whole shebang. At times during *I'd Do Anything*, I'd had a sneaky feeling that Cameron and Andrew might have favoured other hopefuls as Nancy – and in the final, they'd picked my rival as their first choice. You may remember the rumours, too, that Cameron was concerned that I was a little too 'heavy' for the role. In addition, I'd never had a leading role in a West End musical before. All in all, they were taking a big gamble on me.

Yet I was determined that my opening night would be mind-blowing. I needed to prove to these theatrical legends that I *was* their perfect Nancy. I knew I could do it. I knew I could be the Nancy they wanted, even if it had once crossed their minds that I might be too old or too full around the bones.

With just minutes to go before I took to the stage and (hopefully) dazzled in front of the first-night audience and hawk-eyed critics, I started to have second thoughts. Could I really do this?

I glanced at the good-luck cards that I had placed around me on the dressing table for moral support. There were messages from John Barrowman, Andrew Lloyd Webber and Cameron, and a bunch of cards from my mates back home in Blackpool. The most important good-luck messages came from my mum, dad and brother Marko (there was even one from my dogs, written by my mum). They all wished me luck and reassured me that I'd be fabulous on the night.

My family was another reason I was nervous, though. While I was worried what the public, Andrew and Cameron would think, the three opinions I value the most belong to Mum, Dad and Marko. They have been so supportive over the years and helped me to get to where I am: I was terrified that I'd make a show of myself on stage by hitting a bum note, falling arse over tit, or just making a right mess of it all. I was convinced in my heart that I was thoroughly capable of pulling it off, but there is always a chance that things might go wrong.

There was a knock on the door and Alan, the stage manager, gave me my final call. The time had come to put my money where my mouth was. I stood up, feeling a little shaky on my feet.

'Not now, Jodie,' I told myself. 'Keep it together. You can do it.'

I looked at myself in the mirror one last time, all decked out in my Nancy outfit. I looked the part, that's for sure. I gave my reflection a big grin. What did I have to lose? Nothing – apart from my dignity, my job and the respect of my family if it all went horribly tits-up.

I reached for the door handle, twisted it, and stepped into the corridor. I paused for a moment, preparing myself. Then I snaked my way toward the stage, where the show was already in full swing.

Standing in the wings listening for my cue, I could feel my palms begin to sweat and my heart beating heavily in my chest. Once I was out there, I'd be fine. It was just the waiting that was killing me.

I glanced into the sold-out auditorium. Beyond the blinding lights, I knew it was packed tightly, with the eager first-night audience lapping up the fun. Soon all those eyes would be fixed on me. How would I cope? Would I wilt under the intense gaze of the crowd, who would be desperate to see if I could pull it off?

'Pull yourself together, Jodie,' I told myself over and over. 'You've faced tougher challenges than this before. This one is nothing.'

And then it was time. My cue was coming up. Taking a deep breath, I took the plunge and stepped out on to the stage …

1

Reality Bites

Now, you're possibly thinking to yourself, it's understandable for Jodie to be crippled by first-night nerves. After all, it's undoubtedly a big deal for someone who's won a talent show to tread the same boards as West End veterans, especially under the watchful eyes of musical-theatre gods like Lloyd Webber and Mackintosh.

But I am an old hand at this entertainment lark. Fair enough, I'd never really made it big or worked the theatre circuit in London, but I had certainly earned my place in *Oliver!* over the years.

If there's one thing I'd hate for people to think, it's that I've had it easy; that winning *I'd Do Anything* gave me this miraculous chance to do something I'd always dreamed of without having to work for it. That couldn't be further from the truth. Sure, I'd always thought about starring in one of those lavish musicals you see when you head down to the big smoke. I'd loved the idea of entertaining hundreds of theatregoers every night. But I never expected it to land in my lap.

For some people, taking part in a reality show is considered the worst thing a person can do. Those participating are seen as fame-hungry piss-takers who presume the world will fall at their feet.

Just look at those silly sods who appear on *Big Brother*. I'm not knocking them or anything, because they do have their place in the grand scheme of things, and some of them are lovely (for example, Alison Hammond), but tell me – what is it any of them are famous for? Sitting on a couch picking their nose? Having an argument with someone over an Oxo cube? Or bonking a footballer? As far as I can see, none of them go on the programme to change the world or to show off any kind of talent. They're more preoccupied with getting their faces in the papers, making money from magazine deals and trying to become a pop star or a WAG. I'll probably get smacked with a Burberry handbag for saying that, but it's true.

I read somewhere recently that kids these days see shows like *The X Factor* and think making it big is easy. They reckon that if you just rock up to an audition and belt out a song, whether you sing well or not, you are guaranteed a bit of fame and bucketloads of cash. I mean, what happened to the days when youngsters wanted to become doctors or teachers? Now the boys want to become footballers and the girls want to marry them.

That's not me. I grew up in a time when you had to work hard to get what you wanted. I was taught that things didn't just happen overnight. When I was growing up in the eighties, there was no *Big Brother* or *X Factor* to look to as an escape route. If you wanted to make it big, you had to graft and you had to graft hard.

Not that that would make it any easier. After all, how many hopefuls ever managed to make their dream come true? Especially kids up north, who were led to believe that London was the place where opportunity reigned.

I was lucky. I lived in Blackpool, the showbiz mecca of the north. The home of the summer season, donkeys, and fish and chips. It was where old family favourites like Little and Large and Cannon and Ball – and some not-so-family-friendly turns like Bernard Manning and Roy Chubby Brown – had holidaymakers in stitches. Growing up in those surroundings, it was pretty inevitable that I'd fancy myself as an entertainer one day. I guess there must have been something in that sea air.

But it wasn't that I wanted to become famous. I wasn't all that arsed about wanting to be like the people I read about in magazines and newspapers, who had to fend off the paparazzi day in and day out. Graham Norton once said that becoming famous is a fluke and I believe that.

All I wanted was to entertain folks. As soon as I could speak and walk, I used to love singing and dancing and dressing up, and the buzz I got from seeing people enjoying what I did was addictive. If I could put a smile on someone's face, that was all that mattered.

And so, for the next twenty-seven years or so, I worked bloody hard. Harder than you could ever imagine. It wasn't an easy ride – oh no, it was one tough slog. But hey, it was fun along the way and those years have made me truly thankful that I've finally reached a point in my life where I can say to myself, 'Yes, I've made it.'

Let me tell you, that sounded good in my head ... but it looks even better written down in black and white: I've made it.

2
The Little Miracle

When I entered the world, on 12 June 1979, it came as something of a relief to my parents, Madeleine and Marty Prenger.

No, I wasn't a particularly heavy baby – in fact, it was the lightest I've been in my entire life, ha ha. I was actually a pretty average 7 lb 7 oz. Talk about deceptive, eh? The reason why my birth came as such a welcome relief to my parents was that I was like their little miracle. At least, that's how I like to think of myself.

You see, Mum and Dad had discovered early on in their marriage that they couldn't conceive a child. No matter how hard they tried, nothing seemed to work. It was heartbreaking for them to have to deal with, because they both had so much love to give.

Desperate to start a family, they decided to seek medical advice, and headed to Manchester to consult with a specialist. My mum was given the once-over and was advised to take some fertility pills – but was warned that doing so could lead to multiple births. This didn't bother Mum or Dad in the slightest. They were so keen to have children that they didn't mind if they had one, two, three or a hundred little rug rats running around the place. Mum and Dad had enough love to give a small army and they couldn't wait to be parents.

(However, in retrospect – seeing how much of a handful I turned out to be – my mum always jokes that she's glad there was just the one baby at that point in time.

'Can you imagine having to look after five Jodies?' she's exclaimed time and time again. 'I'd be in me grave!')

Mum thought it might take a year or two before she and Dad would see any results – and so, reluctantly, she put the idea of being a mother to the back of her mind. Yet not long after she started the course of pills, Mum discovered to her utter shock that she was pregnant.

The doctor called with the results one afternoon. Wonderfully, he broke the news by singing 'Thank Heaven for Little Girls' down the phone to my mum, who was over the moon to find out that she was expecting the baby she had longed for.

Dad, of course, had still to be told. Upon learning that he was to be a father, he swept Mum into his arms and spun her around – before putting her down again suddenly as he thought he might hurt the baby. Neither of them could believe how fast the treatment had worked.

With hardly time for a breath, Mum set about planning for the baby. She headed straight to Mothercare to start buying bits and bobs for her bundle of joy. In truth, she might as well have bought shares in the company – because Mum being Mum, she wanted to have the nursery fit for a princess. Stuff that ... a queen.

When she discovered a while later that her first-born would indeed be of the fairer sex, she was beside herself.

'I was so excited,' my mum always tells me. 'I was so looking forward to dressing up my little girl just like me.' Which is exactly what she did – but more of that later.

Though Mum knew the sex of the baby, she decided to keep my dad in the dark so that he had a surprise to look forward to on the day of the birth. Of course, if he had been canny, he probably could have guessed from the stuff Mum was buying exactly which gender baby they were going to have.

On 12 June 1979, Mum checked herself into the Blackpool Victoria Hospital to be induced. As well as having gone past her due date, she had high blood pressure, so the doctors wanted to kick-start proceedings.

The day had finally arrived: the day on which Mum would at last become the mother she'd always hoped she'd be. But, while she might have been looking forward to this transformation all her life, she had some serious second thoughts as she lay on the hospital bed with her feet in stirrups trying to squeeze me out. Why? Because, she tells me, the experience was not – how shall I put this? – the most pleasant.

My mum had decided to pay for private treatment at the hospital as that was the only way, in those days, that you could get access to consultants. So, she had all the comforts going. Nevertheless, they couldn't numb the pain of this process and, let me tell you, I seemed to make sure there was a lot of pain.

According to Mum, I wasn't that keen on coming out. Every time they thought I was going to stick my head out, I'd turn around and wedge myself in. I just kept rotating round and round and round. My mum reckons I wasn't coming out until I had my make-up on!

This to-ing and fro-ing went on for quite a while – so long, in fact, that Dr Aird suggested to Dad that perhaps he should nip out to have a cigarette. Talk about waving a red rag to a bull: my poor mum was having none of it. If she had to go through this unmerciful pain, then so did my dad. Wisely, he stayed put.

Fed up with waiting any longer for me to arrive, the doctor eventually said to my mum: 'We'll get Neville Barnes to help the birth.'

Even though she was in agony, my mum was ready for a fight.

'Neville Barnes?' she screeched. 'We're paying you privately: *you're* going to finish this, not Neville Barnes!'

My mum didn't realize until she saw for herself that 'Neville Barnes' were the forceps that would be used to help me into the world. After eleven hours of pushing and shoving, I finally made my rather late arrival. And despite all the pain I had caused Mum (some forty-seven stitches' worth, in fact), she scooped me into her arms and fell in love with me straight away. 'You were the most beautiful baby I had ever seen,' she's told me since.

Nevertheless, she swore afterwards that as the birth had been so hard, she'd never ever go through it all again.

As she held me in her arms for the first time, my mum admired the lovely bronzed tint I had to my skin, and proudly pointed out my olive complexion to the nurses. She was told I had jaundice. My poor mum was gutted; soon afterwards, I turned into a regular pink baby.

My dad was overwhelmed by my arrival. It was like a baby had never been born before. He idolized me from that very day – and still does. He really would do anything for me.

Mum thinks he spoiled me rotten when I was growing up, but then I was his little girl. It was his job. And to tell you the truth, my mum was just as bad.

3

The Ballad of Ma and Pa Prenger

Mum and Dad are without a doubt the best parents any kid could ask for. I know most kids say that, but in this case, it's absolutely true. Funny, caring, loving ... if there was a prize for the best parents in history, then they'd win it hands down.

What's more amazing is that they've been madly and happily in love ever since they first met almost thirty-five years ago. Yet if it hadn't been for a trip to Canada, their paths might never have crossed.

They started life oceans apart as it was. My dad was born in Gramsbergen, Holland, while Mum came into the world in Manchester, England. Dad's whole family – my oma and opa, and his two brothers and three sisters – emigrated to Canada when Dad was a child, to farm the land there and begin a new life. They soon settled and took Canadian nationality.

Bizarrely enough, when my mum was six, her dad (my beloved granddad) decided that a similar course might suit them. He thought life might be more fruitful if they moved to Australia. At that time in the late 1950s, everyone from England was moving Down Under. It was like the promised land – but not as far as my nan was concerned. She didn't want to uproot herself and move across the world from the place she'd grown up.

After some heated conversations, they decided to cut their losses, sell up in Manchester and head to Blackpool, where they launched themselves into the hotel business, snapping up a picturesque B&B called Mount Pleasant. (You know, I can't believe they got away with calling a B&B 'Mount Pleasant' – mind you, things were different in those days.)

Not all of Nan's family decided against emigration, though. Nan's brother, my mum's Uncle Joe, took the boat to Canada on a £10 passage, with a plan to work in the Pickle Crow Gold Mines. Later, he ran a hotel in Thunder Bay, Ontario, called Adanac (that's 'Canada' spelt backwards).

As you might have already guessed, when she was about twenty-two, Mum decided to visit him. She saw the trip as a way to see a bit of the world. As much as she enjoyed living in Blackpool, it was small and everyone knew everyone else's business. Plus, off-season, it was pretty much a ghost town. To head out overseas was an exhilarating adventure, even if it meant leaving her parents behind for a time, which – as Mum was an only child – was a big deal. Indeed, despite Mum's excitement, Nan was forlorn as she watched her only child jetting off to a different continent.

Within days of her arrival in Canada, Mum made friends with some of the girls at the Adanac and they spent many nights hopping from one bar to the next. It was in one of these bars that Mum and Dad met for the first time. Neither can remember who made the first move, but when they did finally come together to chat, they hit it off straight away.

Initially, they hung out with each other as friends, but it wasn't long before romance blossomed. Over the next four months, the pair of them did what boyfriends and girlfriends do: enjoyed every minute of each other. The intensity of their relationship was deepened by the fact that they knew they didn't have long together.

You see, Mum planned to stay out in Canada for only a few months. After that, she felt obliged to return home again to her folks. And in truth, although she was having a gay old time of it with Dad, she was missing home terribly and she longed to see her parents again. Yet, at the same time, in her heart she wanted to be with my dad. She was sure she had found The One. But he lived all the way on the other side of the Atlantic Ocean. The budding romance seemed doomed.

When the day finally came for Mum to head back to Blackpool, she was heartbroken, as it meant that she would have to say goodbye to the man she had fallen in love with. All the way home she thought about Dad, about all the good times they'd shared and how much she was going to miss him.

By the time she touched down in England, she had made a decision. She wanted to be with him and if that meant she had to uproot herself and head back to Thunder Bay, then so be it.

Of course, Mum had only just come home. There could be no travelling again for a while. Luckily, my dad was just as smitten, and soon came over to England for a visit, albeit an all-too-brief one.

When they were apart, it was hard. Mum and Dad used to record tapes for each other – Dictaphone-style recordings of them telling each other how they felt. These would be mailed across the miles and received as preciously as traditional love letters.

After a couple of months of trying to fit back into Blackpool life, Mum finally had enough. She had to be with Marty – and that meant moving to Canada. Nan was devastated, but she had to trust that Mum knew what she was doing. The journey to the airport was dreadful, with tears flowing freely. Once there, Mum says that she could see that her departure was breaking her parents' hearts.

It wasn't easy for her to leave. Her folks had given her a good life, but she had found Mr Right. How could she risk losing that for ever, never knowing if she'd find someone as perfect in Blackpool?

Shortly after her return to Canada, her Uncle Joe sadly passed away, so she went to live with my dad and his family on their farm. It wasn't the kind of farm that we're used to over here, with the smell of cow dung in the air. It was a massive place with acres of land, where they bred Arabian horses. It was beautiful, but Mum never settled there. She kept thinking about home, and about her parents, who were no doubt worrying about how she was. Dad, of course, picked up on her sadness, but she reassured him time and time again that she was happy and keen to stay put. By now, she couldn't bear to be without him.

To pass the time, she got herself a job in a beauty salon at a department store called Eatons. As she loved make-up, and making herself and others look gorgeous, the work really helped to take her mind off missing England. Yet when each day was over, waves of homesickness would wash over her again.

Dad tried his best to make Mum feel at home, but he knew that there was something wrong. In the end, she couldn't lie to him and confessed all – and in response, Dad told Mum that he was happy to move to Blackpool, so that they could start a new life together. Mum was stunned. She couldn't believe that he was willing to sacrifice his life for her, to leave his family and friends, just to make her happy. Now that's true love.

Really, Mum shouldn't have been all that surprised about the strength of Dad's feelings. During their time together in Canada, he had presented her with a friendship ring, which is considered to be a kind of pre-engagement ring there. So Mum had known in advance that Dad was serious about her. All the same, to learn that he was willing to make such a commitment to her, to move across an ocean, made her feel like she was on top of the world.

Needless to say, Nan and Granddad were overjoyed when their daughter finally arrived home, two years after she'd vanished from their sight, and they soon fell in love with the man who had caused all the trouble. Dad is easy to fall in love with. Just ask anyone who's met him and they will say he is the nicest guy you could meet. He hasn't got a bad bone in his body; he's so laid back, he's practically horizontal. He's the kind of man who, if you went to him and told him, 'The world is going to end in two minutes,' he'd be like, 'Oh right, okay.'

Not that I want to go on, but he's an unselfish man.

Eight months after my folks got home, they followed my grandparents and Uncle Joe into the hotel business, opening the Hollies Hotel on Albert Road. It was the heyday of Blackpool hoteliers, and my parents joined the club.

About the same time, Dad proposed to Mum. Down on one knee, he said to her, 'We're obviously going to settle over here, so I want to make my life where yours is.' Without a moment's hesitation, she said yes.

Thirteen months later, they got married in an emotional ceremony at the Sacred Heart Church in Blackpool. The day was a fabulous one with tears and, of course, lots of laughter. Mum's parents looked on with pride as their only daughter became a bride.

It was 17 January 1976: three and a half years before I came along.

4

Born Gobby

I f you've ever wondered where my name – Jodie Christine Prenger – came from, the boring version is that Mum got the idea from a niece they had in Canada on my dad's side, who was called Jodie (the Americanization of Judith). Christine is my mum's middle name, so that explains that.

Yet I prefer the story that my name was written in the stars. Or, more accurately, a fortune-teller's tea leaves …

Just before I was born, Mum went to see a gypsy, who told her, 'You will have two children, but there will be a big gap between them. Your daughter's name will be linked to a religious person. All I can see is a stage and people applauding.'

Now, if you think about it, my name isn't too far off 'Jesus Christ', is it? Jodie Christine. J-Christ, if you were to shorten it, 'J-Lo style'. I bet you're thinking: what a load of old codswallop.

Once I'd arrived, though, there was something more unholy than holy about all the noise I made. If you thought I had a gob on me now with my endless jabbering, you wouldn't believe the racket I made back then. I must have been a terror of a baby because Mum and Dad said I didn't let them get any sleep. I was up *all* the time.

The only way they could get me to shut up was to take me out in the car until I dozed off. Then Mum and Dad would creep back into the hotel and gently place me in my cot. No sooner had they set me down than my eyes would spring open like a doll's; I must have been like Chucky out of *Child's Play* in those first few months.

Nevertheless, to Mum and Dad, I was their precious little gem. They fretted over me so much. It was hard for them because, although they hated to be apart from me, when they were busy in the hotel, they had to entrust me to close friends. There were a couple of girls at the hotel who would look after me. One was Aideen, who became like a second mum to me, and the other was Roseanne. And it was Roseanne who was partly responsible for the day my parents thought I had become the girl out of *The Exorcist*.

It was a sunny day and Roseanne had taken me out to enjoy the sunshine and the fresh air of Blackpool. Bearing in mind I was barely one year old, the scenery was a bit lost on me. I guess all I wanted to do at that age was to be back at home, playing with my rattle or causing havoc with crayons. During our stroll, Roseanne decided to treat me to a tasty mint ice cream, which I demolished in record time. See, my love of sweet things started at a very early age.

Once we got home, Roseanne handed me back to Mum and I sat on the floor in my pretty dress and a pair of white tights. All of a sudden, there was the most hideous squelching sound and my lovely white tights turned an alarming green colour. My mum looked at me in horror. What was happening to her little girl? It was, she recalls, just like that scene in *The Exorcist* when Linda Blair vomits up the pea soup.

In a panic, Mum called Doctor Twenty Quid, a locum who would come out to see folks around the clock whenever you asked him to. Within minutes, he arrived at the hotel, expecting to have to admit me to hospital to undergo urgent tests to determine exactly what had shot out of me and in such a grotesque way.

He quickly gave me the once-over, and then turned to my mum gravely. For an instant, she thought bad news was on its way, but then Dr Twenty Quid's face burst into a broad smile and he said: 'Madeleine, my love, Jodie is just fine. From what I can see, she has had a little too much mint ice cream, that's all.'

Yes, the icky green muck was in fact the ice cream I'd lapped up earlier in the day: it had literally shot right through me. The relief on my mum's face, Dad tells me, was a picture.

It was around this time that I first showed the world that I had singing promise – of sorts. I have my Aunty Olga to thank for that.

Olga wasn't really my aunty. She wasn't a blood relative at all, but by God she was definitely one of the family. She had worked for my nan at her hotel for thirty years and was a real asset. She often looked after me and taught me to sing songs like 'D.I.S.C.O.' I used to love singing with her. Olga would stand me on the kitchen table and get me to trill out a number. 'Sexy Eyes' was a favourite and when I sang it, I'd blink my lashes at her. Olga was a love and she looked after me as if I were her own.

With a gob like mine, once I'd been taught a few melodies, I would sing them everywhere and anywhere. Sometimes Mum would bathe me in the kitchen sink and, like the camp diva I would grow up to be, I'd demand to be covered in bubbles while I sang away, as if I didn't have a care in the world. But then again, aged one I probably didn't. Those worries would come later.

Whenever I could, I would show off. Or, as I prefer to see it, I'd practise for the career at which I would one day excel. Before one, I was able to walk, and my mum was very proud of that achievement. She used to throw big birthday parties for friends and family, and she'd invite all the girls who had had babies around the same time as her. While all the other one-year-olds were crawling around on the floor, I would be running about the place like an athlete. My mum always had such a big smile on her face because of that.

When it came to talking, Mum says that she can't remember what my first words were – though she is sure that they were something like, 'Can I have ...' Whatever phrase it was, one thing is certain: once I started speaking, I never stopped. In fact, Mum reckons I'm probably still on the same breath.

As I got older, I gained more confidence and became even more of a show-off. In particular, I loved prancing about the hotel, where we lived in the basement flat for the first years of my life. The Hollies Hotel was a purpose-built building, with about forty bedrooms across five floors. Mum and Dad bought the adjoining hotel too and that made room for a huge bar area. It was there that I would stand by the brown coffee machine and just babble on about nothing. Soon, dressing up in fancy frocks and hanging out in the lounge with the guests became my *raison d'être*. The guests enjoyed my appearances and they seemed to find me funny, which thrilled me to my core.

Mum tells me that I always wanted to be around people. Even though I was a relatively shy child at heart, I relished talking to the guests. It was funny: I used to hide behind Mum when it came to meeting new people when we were out and about, yet when I was dressed up and singing or dancing in front of everyone, I would lord it all over the place and bathe in the attention.

My mum says I was like my nan. She used to do the same. She was the entertainer of the family. She'd throw on her glad rags and lip sync her way through some old Shirley Bassey classics for the guests and they'd love it. She was brilliant and she had everyone lapping up her performance. I really admired that.

Nan and Granddad lived just across the road from us. All my memories of them are special. They were the kindest, most loving people you could ever meet. Whenever I threw a tantrum with Mum and Dad, I only had to run across the street to see them and they would mop up my tears and make sure I was all right. They put up with a lot from me, but they knew I loved them with all my heart.

Like Mum, Nan was a strong woman. Life hadn't always been easy for Terri Quinn. She grew up in Manchester with her nine siblings; she was the youngest, but ended up having to deal with a lot. When she was just nine years old, she discovered her mum dead in the fireplace. It later emerged that she had had an epileptic fit and fallen into the fire, banging her head on the way down, which had killed her instantly. Nan was devastated. After that, she was brought up by her older sister Mary.

Years later, Nan got a job in a cafe where all the Manchester United Busby Babes used to hang out. She dated one of them, but would never tell me who, even after much persuasion – to this day, I still don't know. That cafe was also where she met my granddad, Jack, who at the time was a plumber, though of course they went on to open their hotel.

I didn't see my dad's parents so much when I was growing up. Oma and Opa, as I called them, lived in Canada, so it wasn't a matter of just dropping by. We spoke on the phone frequently and there was the odd visit. They were very religious. Every mealtime, Oma would read from the Bible before we ate, which I found very confusing when I was young. I simply didn't understand why we had to have a story when there was food to be devoured!

When I was three, Mum and Dad tried to send me to Happy Lands, the local nursery. Big mistake. Instead of experiencing a calm and peaceful introduction to nursery life, I made sure there was a drama of epic proportions. No sooner had I walked through the door, I was screaming like a flaming banshee and grabbing on to Mum. I was so loud that I wouldn't be surprised if they had heard my yelling all the way down in London.

I don't know why I was such a Little Miss Temper Tantrum. The other kids seemed all right and the teacher looked quite nice too. But I wasn't having any of it. I didn't want to be there. Full stop. And I made sure that everyone – and I mean everyone – knew how I felt.

Mum and Dad tried to calm me down and told me that if I gave it a chance, I could make lovely new friends and play fun games. But all I wanted was to be back home in my familiar surroundings. In spite of my wailing, Mum and Dad refused to listen, so I had no choice but to pull out the big guns and really make them feel guilty.

I told the pair of them that I had a sore head, that my tummy was aching, that I had a pain in my tooth … I tried every trick in the book. And guess what? They bought it. Or so I thought. In retrospect, I think they were probably so ashamed of my behaviour that they thought it was best to get me home before I cracked the windows with my shrill cries.

While I was busy making a show of myself, Mum looked at Dad and told him to put me in the car. Once he'd done that, he went back to the nursery and paid a full week's fee to avoid arguments. Miraculously, on the way home, all of my aches and pains disappeared. Weird, that. My mum remembers that I snuggled up to her and said thoughtfully, 'Maybe some other kid can go instead of me.'

Later on, I ended up attending a Salvation Army playgroup a few days a week: an arrangement with which I – and they – could just about cope.

5

In Sickness and in Sums

At four, I started at a nearby school called Langdale. Being three foot at the time, it felt like the biggest place in the world to me. In fact, it wasn't one of those large schools that you see in the major cities, with a sprawling complex of numerous buildings. It was basically just two semi-detached houses joined together, which had been converted into a handful of classrooms. When I walk past it these days, it seems so very small. But then, that happens when you get older.

It was at Langdale that I made some of my earliest friends, like Natalie Bryan, Laura Stone, Natalie Middlemiss, Gemma Rowland and Emma Rathbone. We're all still pals today, partly because we had such a ball at school. Well, some of the time.

Langdale certainly wasn't a holiday camp, that's for sure. As with most things in life, there was a downside to the fun. That downside came in the form of Mrs Flemming. Now, if I said she reminded me of a witch, I wouldn't be exaggerating. She had this huge mop of wiry red hair that was so wild and unruly that it actually looked like someone had set her tresses on fire and forgotten to blow them out. She cut a terrifying figure as she stomped around the school, like she was on a hunt for a little kid whom she could turn into a frog. She was the kind of woman you'd expect to find in your worst nightmares. On occasion, I did.

It is because of Mrs Flemming that I have a fear of my times table, which we began to learn almost from the very first day. Even now, just hearing a number being multiplied by another is enough to send a shiver right through me. In lessons, Mrs Flemming would make one of the class get up in front of everyone and recite the times table. Let me repeat: in front of *everyone*.

Of course, if it was me, I'd stumble over the sums and make mistakes and not be able to work out the answers in my head. Basically, I'd look like a prize banana. What else was likely to happen when I was trying so hard not to slip up and look stupid under the gaze of thirty-odd kids, not to mention the icy stare of Mrs Flemming?

Slip up I did, sometimes in a major way. I felt I always came away looking like a dumb-ass. It was frustrating because, believe me, I'm not stupid in any sense of the word. I just really struggled to learn my times table.

Fortunately, Mrs Flemming wasn't the only teacher at the school. If she was the Wicked Witch of the West, then her colleague Mrs Helm was Glinda, the Good Witch of the South. In fact, it's unfair even to call her a witch. With her long white hair, she looked more like an angel, and was such a contrast to Mrs Flemming, in that she was nice, considerate and friendly. I have lovely memories of her to this day.

Langdale was just on the corner of our road, so every lunchtime my mum would pick me up and take me back home for a bite to eat. That way, she hoped there would be no repeat of my nursery performance. Yet despite those lunchtime sessions, I used to cause a right stink when it came to going to school – partly because of Witch Flemming's iron rule and partly because I just hated being away from my mum.

As I had with nursery, I tried every trick in the book to get out of attending. I used to bite myself to make myself cry, or I'd come up with ingenious ways of making myself seem sick. One method was to put talc on my face to create a deathly pale visage, while another was to press my face against the radiator and then tell my mum that I was feeling feverish. Some of the time she'd believe me and I'd get to stay home, but Mum was no fool and it wasn't long before she wised up to my tricks.

Naturally, there were the odd occasions when – just like the boy who cried wolf – I actually did fall ill. Such as the time I was sick with pneumonia, when I was five. I came home from school one afternoon and lay down on the couch. Before I knew it, I was in the Land of Nod.

As I snoozed, Mum noticed that my breathing had become irregular and that I appeared to be reciting my times tables in my sleep. Yes, the times tables I couldn't do in class, I could perform in a pneumonic slumber! Go figure. When my mum felt my forehead, she discovered that I was burning up – and not because I had pressed my head against a radiator. This time, it was for real.

Sensing something was amiss, Mum got straight on the phone to Dr Twenty Quid. His advice was to strip me and put me straight to bed. The next morning, I was still poorly and my face was covered in pneumonic spots. A pretty sight I was not. My mum was advised to keep me at home for the duration of my illness: the doctors thought I'd be more comfortable that way, rather than taking me to hospital.

Soon after, they discovered that I had a shadow on my lung. A specialist was called and he gave me the treatment I needed. I was really sick for well over a month. Even afterwards, I had to have chest X-rays every three months for the next two years, until I was seven. Luckily – as everyone has heard for themselves – the shadow didn't damage my lungs in any way: I can still belt out ballads with the best of 'em.

When I wasn't being ill, I was being a right clumsy mare. I was the kind of girl who could walk in a straight line and still end up in A & E with a saucepan on my head. That, strangely, never actually happened, but I did suffer more than my fair share of cuts and scrapes.

One time, when I was showing off at the hotel, I ended up losing my four front teeth. I was with this girl called Megan, who worked at the hotel and who I really disliked. I don't know why I did, but she just bugged me – which at my young age was reason enough. Whenever she was around me, I'd pull really horrible faces behind her back and generally be a not-very-nice girl.

On this particular day, I was standing by the serviette cupboard when Megan walked by. I was dressed up in a pinny for some reason, and was passing the time being silly and pretending I was a little madam. As Megan passed me, I gave her the tongue, as usual, and then proceeded to take off my pinny.

But, as I did so, I stood on the bottom of the apron, got caught up in it, found myself drastically off-balance, and then hurtled face first into the cupboard, smashing my front teeth straight out of my mouth. The pain was excruciating. The scream that came from my lips was so bloodcurdling and loud it would have terrified Yvette Fielding from *Most Haunted*. It hurt. A *lot*.

And the result? Well, four missing teeth, blood across my face and a rather disturbing likeness to a prepubescent Dracula. Only my fangs remained at the front. Oh, it was my worst nightmare.

Well, I say that. Being stuck in a lift with Mrs Flemming might have been far worse.

6

Dancing Queen

When I turned five, I decided that I wanted to be a dancer. Not a surprising decision considering that most five-year-old girls want to be the same thing, but in my case it was what you'd call a brave choice, bearing in mind that at this stage I wasn't exactly the size of a beanpole.

Let's get this straight. From the age of three, when I was already a plump child, I put on a stone every birthday – so even by five years old, I was really quite heavy, especially when compared to other children my age.

While I might not have been light on my feet in a literal sense, I was still a pretty nifty mover who could throw a few shapes. As a result, Mum kindly took me along to some local dance classes.

I was really excited; I couldn't wait to learn tap and ballet. I had fallen in love with the idea of gliding across the floor like the dancers in the film *A Chorus Line.* Of course, I'd forgotten that most of those light-footed dynamos were actually that – light-footed.

When I arrived in class for the first time, dressed head to toe in my Lycra combo (you're right, it wasn't pretty), I felt giddy with anticipation. The reality proved not to be as fulfilling as I'd hoped. Not only did I try to do tap steps in my ballet slippers – so *that*'s why I couldn't hear anything – I was also the butt of everyone's jokes. Apparently, Lycra just isn't a good look for anyone who is 'big boned'. You don't say. I was five and fashion wasn't even on my radar, but the nasty comments from the other kids still affected me. How could they be so mean? And why were they?

To be laughed at and picked on by my fellow students was unbearable. At that age, I didn't have a bad bone in my body. Just because all my good bones were covered in several layers of flesh, they felt they had a free pass to make me feel awful.

Every time I went to class and got laughed at, I'd go home and tell Mum what had happened. She told me later that she was heartbroken for me. It's not nice for any mother to hear that their child is unpopular, and she certainly didn't want to see me upset. As most parents would do in that situation, she went to see the teacher to have a word with her about the bullying. Yet Mum's pleading fell on deaf ears. Kids can be cruel ... so too can adults, as it turned out.

The teacher was as bad as the rest of the class and told my mum that it was probably better for everyone if I went and found something that was more suited to me; that I should give dance the big heave-ho. She said that she wanted me to leave. I was 'too weighty to dance', apparently, and she reckoned that I was not only wasting my own time, but hers too.

What a flaming cheek! I may have been somewhat fuller-figured than the other students, but I was a great little mover on the dance floor. I certainly had rhythm, and what I lacked in grace, I more than made up for in energy and style. My teacher may not have seen my potential, but regardless of my size, I knew I could do it if I put my mind to it.

That night, Mum came home and told me that my dance classes were no more. As parents do, she spared my feelings by spinning me a white lie that the school had closed down. Which, when you think about it, is pretty much like telling a kid that their dog has gone to stay on their uncle's farm, when in fact it is as dead as a doornail. The news (whatever the truth of it) was devastating to me. All my dreams of going to the Royal Ballet School – as misguided as they were – were dashed.

Yet I wasn't defeated: if I wasn't allowed to dance, then I would try something else instead. Like acting, perhaps. A year or so later, it was announced that our school was going to put on a pantomime, and I jumped at the chance to take part. All I could think about was dressing up as Cinderella or the Sleeping Beauty.

Once again, though, the fairy-tale ending escaped me: when I turned up at the auditions, I was told that I had landed the role of the tree, which would stand at the back of the stage for the entire production.

Gutted isn't the word. I had so wanted a speaking role and, as far as I knew, there were no great speaking trees. Unless they were barking mad (ahem). Nevertheless, a role was a role and so I accepted it graciously, even though inside I was absolutely fizzing.

When I went home to tell my mum, she told me she was very proud of me. You know, I'm sure she was trying to stifle her laughter. I can remember her telling me that she'd always thought I would make a good oak.

Despite Mum's stifled giggles on this occasion, my parents were generally so kind and loving that I couldn't imagine being without them – which is perhaps another reason why I never wanted to go to school. Why would I want to, when the alternative was to stay at the hotel with people who loved me with all their hearts?

Speaking of schools, it was time for me to change institutions. Like most female students at Langdale, at the age of seven my mates and I moved on to Elmslie Girls' School, which wasn't too far away from home. It was bigger than Langdale, but the roll accommodated only 500 girls, ranging from age four to eighteen, which meant classes were small.

The school was set in a beautiful, ornate Victorian house, and had taken its name from the huge elm tree that had been in the garden when it first opened. Purple and yellow flowers had surrounded the tree, and these went on to become the school colours.

As usual, my first day there was full of drama. Mum and Dad got me up and dressed in my new violet uniform at the crack of dawn. I was nervous, as school still wasn't one of my favourite things to do. I would have preferred to stay at the hotel with Mum. But, quite rightly, she told me that I had to go to school whether I liked it or not.

Consequently – albeit reluctantly – I agreed to attend, but when we turned up at the school gates, something was odd. Elmslie appeared to be deserted. There wasn't a soul to be seen.

We checked the time. We were right on schedule, but nonetheless there was no one around. Had they all heard that I was on my way and run off, for fear that I'd eat them or sit on them? We flagged down a passing caretaker, and were told – reassuringly, but embarrassingly – that we were a full twenty-four hours early for the first day. D'oh!

The following morning, I returned to find the place full of children. I knew there and then that I wasn't going to like my new school all that much and I told my mum that I didn't want to go back. But of course, despite my protestations, I did. Again and again.

Mum must have despaired that I'd never grow out of my phase of hating to be away from the comforts of home. Yet there was one occasion, after I had joined the Brownies, when Mum believed that I'd come round to the idea at last.

I was seven and, for the first time since my doomed dancing classes, in the Brownies I had found something that I enjoyed doing. I was completely oblivious to the fact that when I wore my traditional brown uniform, I looked like a big poo.

You should have seen my parents' faces when I enthusiastically told them that our Brownie troupe was heading off to Sheffield for a three-day residential trip. They were shocked because, up until this point, I had found it difficult to be apart from them for a mere matter of hours. Now here I was informing them that I was looking forward to spending three whole days away from my family. They couldn't believe it.

On the morning of my big adventure, my mum packed a suitcase with enough stuff for an around-the-world tour. As I climbed on the coach and waved goodbye to Mum, I was all excited about heading out of Blackpool on my own and discovering what lay in other places. I told myself that it was good for me to see another part of the world, even if it was just Sheffield.

The journey down the motorway was typical as far as Brownie experiences go: we trilled out the good ole 'Kumbaya' and 'Ten Green Bottles', and coupled the singsong with a few games of I Spy – until we ran out of things beginning with 'R'. There are only so many times you can guess 'road'.

Once we arrived at our destination, the games turned to telling ghost stories. Hearing about all the creepy ghoulies sent shivers down my spine. The fact that the tales could actually be true, meanwhile, sent me right over the edge.

At that very moment, back home in Blackpool, Mum and Dad were settled on the sofa in their flat at the hotel, enjoying their first night in without Jodie getting under their feet and thanking their lucky stars that they had a peaceful night's sleep ahead of them. Oh, if only they knew.

Long after they'd turned in, at around 1 a.m., the phone suddenly sprang into life. It was Brown Owl on the line – and she didn't sound happy.

'Mrs Prenger,' she said, 'would you kindly come and fetch your daughter, please?'

It turned out that those 'real-life' reports of the paranormal – paired with the fright of finding a big fat spider in my bed – had turned me into a nervous wreck: one that couldn't be calmed down, despite Brown Owl's best attempts. And so my poor dad had to throw on his clothes and drive with

Mum through the night down to Sheffield, where they found a sobbing Jodie who was desperate to leave camp. When I saw them, I ran into their arms and begged to be taken home.

Plonking me on the back seat, Dad drove us all the way back to Blackpool, arriving at the hotel at 5.30 a.m., just in time for the two of them to start preparing breakfasts for the fifty-odd guests who were staying at the time.

My parents are like no others, bless 'em. They really would lay down their lives for me.

7
Oh, Brother!

For almost eight years, the Prenger household revolved around one person: Jodie. In that time, I definitely made my mark. I sang, I danced, I ate and I also threw one or two paddies along the way.

Still, in spite of it all, Mum and Dad loved me. I was their only child, their golden princess. They spoiled me rotten, just like many parents do when they have only one kid on whom to focus their attention.

Dad was like my personal driver. Wherever I wanted to go, he would take me. Even to this day, Mum tells anyone who'll listen that my dad is a pushover with me, but I love him. Mum reckons I sometimes forget that cars have tanks that open. I simply say, 'Dad, there's no petrol in my car,' and it miraculously appears.

Yet my mum also doted on me. Every year, she would transform my bedroom into a little kiddie's palace: the decor changed annually, themed with whatever the cartoon character of the moment was. I recall that I had a Barbie room at one point, and those black-and-white clowns another time (which is mildly creepy in hindsight). She-Ra was in one year, then Rainbow Brite the next. Do you remember Rainbow Brite? I loved her even more than the Care Bears.

Christmas was another special time for lil' old me. It was a real family affair, when Mum and Dad would put the hotel second and us as a family first. We'd decorate the place to look festive, with a new colour scheme each year. We'd adorn the outside of the house with toy Santas, reindeers and snowmen, and bedeck the building with lights. Christmas meant a lot to us and we really went to town when it came to celebrating it.

For Mum and Dad loved Christmas as much as I did. They truly got caught up in the spirit of the season. Their motto was that any excuse to have a good time was a worthy one – and it could come at any time of the year, for that matter, as Mum adored throwing parties. She really was the hostess with the mostess.

But for me, 25 December was the pinnacle of my year. Every time, I'd find so many wonderful presents waiting for me under the tree on Christmas morning. And every year, I'd put out more and more mince pies for Santa, so that he would leave me loads of lovely gifts. I was never disappointed with what I'd find; Mum and Dad were always more than generous.

Yet in the late summer of 1986, a shadow fell over my joy at being this golden child. My position looked threatened when Mum made an unexpected announcement one day.

'Jodie,' she said to me. 'We've got some great news for you. You're going to have a little baby brother or sister.'

'A what?' I asked, shocked and slightly appalled. 'A brother or sister?'

Mum explained, 'I'm going to have a baby. Aren't you excited?'

If I'd known then what I know now, I probably would have said, 'Oh Mum, I am excited. I am so happy. I can't wait to have someone to grow up with.' But at the time, when I was so used to having my own way, I wasn't having any of it.

'Are you sure?' I hedged, hoping Mum was just teasing me.

'Yes,' Mum said. 'I'm quite sure.'

'Oh,' I sighed. 'That's nice.'

Secretly – or perhaps not quite as secretly as I thought – I was seething. I couldn't believe Mum and Dad could have done this to me. Hadn't Mum said after her difficult first pregnancy that kids were off the agenda? How dare they even think about having another child when they already had me? Why on earth did they need one – surely I was more than enough for them to contend with? Yet I knew first-hand that my parents had a lot of love to give; it turned out that, as much as they cherished me, they wanted to have another baby.

'Oh well, so be it,' I thought. There was nothing I could do. But if that new kid thought that he or she could get one over on me, he or she had another think coming. I had the advantage. I had a head start. I'd been part of this family for almost eight years. I wasn't going to let some newbie just crawl into my life, gurgling here and breaking wind there. I was still the golden princess and there was no way I would let any brother or sister steal my throne.

Of course, looking back, they were silly thoughts to have. But when you're used to ruling the roost, it's hard to imagine someone else sharing your life and your parents. For eight years, I had been Mum and Dad's pride and joy. What was life going to be like when my parents were distracted by a noisy, smelly rug rat?

Over the next six months or so, I watched Mum's belly grow bigger and bigger. As the birth date approached, I wondered more about how life would change. It wouldn't, I decided. Life would be just the same. Mum and Dad would still love me as much as they had before. Sure, they'd momentarily be caught up with the new arrival, but it was Jodie whom they had known the longest.

The day of reckoning came on 19 March 1987. It was after school and I was stretched out on the couch watching *He-Man*. Mum was upstairs somewhere and Dad was out shopping. Aunty Aideen was also there, busying herself around the hotel, even though she too was pregnant.

All of a sudden, while He-Man was waving his mighty sword around and declaring, 'By the power of Greyskull!', Mum let out a heroic yell of her own and started calling for me.

'Jodie! Jodie! Get Aideen. Quick! My waters have broken.'

Mesmerized by He-Man's adventure battling the evil Skeletor, I merely tilted my head and called back, 'What was that, Mum?'

'My waters have broken!' Mum shouted. 'Get Aideen now!'

Ah, so that was it. The baby was on its way. Neither excited by the prospect of welcoming in a new life nor angry to have my TV show interrupted, I glanced back at the telly and half-heartedly called out for Aideen. 'Aid? Mum wants you. She's having a baby. Can you be quick, though? *He-Man's* on.'

With that, I went back to watching my cartoon, while Aideen dashed to Mum's aid, prepared her for the hospital and got straight on the phone to Dr Twenty Quid.

By the time he arrived, Mum was in agony, but had still found the presence of mind to slip on her most glamorous fur coat to make herself look presentable. As he guided her out to his car, the doc hesitated.

'What's wrong?' Mum asked, noticing that he had stalled.

'It's just that it's a new set of wheels,' he told her, 'and I don't want my car to be ruined.'

My mum gave him a look that could have stripped paint off a wall. 'Get me to the hospital *now*!' she screamed. 'If I mess your flaming car, I'll buy you a new one.'

With that, Twenty Quid shoved Mum in the back seat and tore off to the Blackpool Victoria Hospital.

This time around, Mum had a much easier time of it than she'd had with me, even though the baby was a whopping 9 lb 10 oz. I rocked up to the hospital around an hour or so later. There was no way I was rushing to see my rival for affection.

According to Mum, I took my time getting ready that day, just like a diva, and I did so in style – sporting a leopard-print dress, if you please. A stunning look, you'll agree, especially when teamed with a dead-straight fringe and a long mullet. Maybe *that*'s where Scary Spice got the idea from ...

The minute I clapped eyes on baby Marko, I fell in love with him. I hadn't wanted to, but it just happened. He was so very beautiful and just perfect in every way: his little nose, his tiny hands that waved in the air, and his little toes that wriggled as I tickled 'em. My steely resolve to resist the urge to be excited – passionately maintained for so many months – dissolved there and then.

Holding all 9 lb 10 oz of him in my arms, I realized that this baby brother was the greatest thing in the world. How could I have thought such terrible things all this while?

Once we got him home, I spent my time helping Mum to change him and look after him. In fact, I was rather excited that I had a new plaything. He was better than any Tiny Tears I'd ever had – except when he went to the loo, when it smelled a tad different to Tiny Tears.

I enjoyed being a sister and I was very protective over him, as I am now. I made sure he was dressed smartly, that he was always in fresh nappies, and I spent hours just stroking his hair. Funny how I thought he'd change the dynamic of the family. Instead, it made the family even better and I realized then, as I still believe now, that I could never live without my gorgeous brother. He's everything to me.

Of course, that's not to say that we don't have our moments getting at each other. What brother and sister don't have the odd spat? That little bugger still manages to rub me up the wrong way, big time.

For as Marko grew older, he worked out ways to antagonize me. Even just playing with each other proved to be a nightmare. Everything I had, he wanted, and some of the things he had, I wanted. He might have been younger than me, but Marko knew how to wind me up good and proper.

One time, I was sitting on the sofa, playing with my keyboard and getting lost in my own musical world. All of a sudden, three-year-old Marko strolled over, waving his plastic sword above his head. The next thing I knew, he started banging my keyboard with it.

Needless to say, I was infuriated and told him to go away, but he continued to pound on the keys. I'll bet Andrew Lloyd Webber never had to put up with that from his brother Julian. I tried to get up to push Marko away – but annoyingly, as I'd been sitting in the seat for so long, I'd actually wedged myself between the cushions, and couldn't move an inch.

Sometimes, I used to negotiate with him: if I sang the *Ninja Turtles* theme tune, would he please leave me alone? On occasion, he did, but more often than not he'd continue to irritate me.

He especially enjoyed rubbing it in that he was the new kid on the block – probably because that was an approach guaranteed to rile me.

So I'd say to him, 'Well, Marko, I have been here longer, so Mum and Dad love me more.'

Then he'd hit back and say, 'Well, I'm more intelligent, so they love me more.'

Our parents would try to calm us down, but we would both throw the question at them, 'Go on, Mum, Dad: which one do you love the most?'

How sad are we? Ah, but we laugh about it now.

My mum and dad love the bones of Marko – just as they do me. But when they started saying that he was the golden child, I wasn't having it.

Cleverly, instead of trying to hide Marko in a drawer or

sell him to a passing salesman, I bargained with my parents. If Marko was going to be known as the golden child, I needed a promotion. I wanted to be the platinum child. Yes, the platinum child. It had a ring to it. And so, from that day on, that's how I was known.

You will probably gather that we're not the normal family; we always love a good laugh. Even the name Marko came from years of me calling my brother 'Marco Polo' and taking the mickey out of him. His name is actually Mark. Even he loves the fact that Marko stuck, though, and that's how he's known to his mates.

Oh, brothers, what are they good for? As Edwyn Starr once said, 'Absolutely nothing.' Or was that about war?

Pah – same thing!

8
She's the Greatest Dancer

Did you happen to notice that description of the dashing outfit I wore to meet my brother for the first time? A leopard-print dress, no less. Perhaps an unusual choice for a child, but I have to confess that it wasn't unusual attire for me. It may have been carefully selected on the day of my brother's birth, but in all honesty I wore that sort of thing day in, day out. My mum's fashion choices for me were always a little ... unorthodox, shall we say.

Because of my ample weight, it was admittedly a challenge to dress me nicely. If you'd seen me waddling down the street, you'd have sworn that I was twenty or thirty years older than I was. Too big for the nice frilly summer dresses that my gal pals could wear, I longed for the day when I could shop at Tammy Girl. Instead, Mum had to raid the shops for women's clothes, to be sure that I'd be able to squeeze into them – and this is definitely not an exaggeration – without ripping the seams.

Frankly, I looked awful. Of course, it didn't help that for part of my childhood my hair was contorted into a hideous scrunch perm – in homage to my idol Michael Jackson – and I wore a pair of massive glasses. I looked like Deirdre frickin' Barlow. Mum loved to dress me in things that she liked, forgetting that she was in her late thirties and I was nine. I was basically a mini Madeleine.

In fairness, it wasn't Mum's fault alone. Nan was just as bad. Whenever she went over to Las Vegas for a holiday, as she did on a regular basis, she'd return home with a bag full of clothes for me. Now think about it. Vegas? Fashion? What do you reckon Nan's style choices were like? You got it: sparkles, shoulder pads and brightly coloured boob tubes. Still, I wore them, even if I did look a bit like a *Dallas* throwback.

To give me some credit, at that time, I really didn't know any better. I grew up when that kind of style was actually fashionable, and was plastered all over the television screens and magazine pages for everyone to emulate.

For apart from the catfights in the lily pond, and the countless bitchy asides, those eighties TV shows were all about glamour and clothes and make-up. Back then, I never really understood that the ostentatious looks of Alexis Carrington, Colby Dexter or S'wellin were also pretty camp. To me, they were women who looked amazing and uber-glam.

Sadly, what was in for Dallas was more like Grimsby for me. Yet at nine years old, and larger than life itself, I wanted the *Dallas* look too – naively not realizing that Joan Collins could pull off wearing those outfits only because she was petite and svelte. I didn't cotton on to the fact that wearing brash outfits in bright colours – I once matched a yellow jumpsuit with a fluffy green shrug – would make me look a million times larger than I was. At the end of the day, I was a young girl and all young girls like to play dress up, even if it is in clothes their mums would look better wearing. The difference in my case was that the clothes didn't ever go back in the box: they were my everyday wardrobe.

I also adored slapping on make-up, which I did well into my twenties. I even – ever the entrepreneur – charged the guests in the hotel 50p a time to do their make-up for them. The sweetest thing was, they always paid me, even though I usually left them looking like dodgy old drag queens.

A year or so after Marko was born, my parents changed

their career. As much as they loved the hotel business, they decided that it was time to do something different. We moved to our own family home on Warbreck Hill Road, and Mum and Dad established a care home for the elderly on Shaftes-bury Avenue, which they run to this day. The work may be hard, but my parents wouldn't swap it for anything else.

The people who come through the home have always been lovely and sweet. In some ways, the old dears who come to stay have become extended family to us all. Many of them really took a shine to me.

I think that's because I'm like an old woman in a young person's body – always have been. You give me a Vera Lynn number and I'll belt it out. You can't beat the old songs, can you? I think I probably got on better with the residents than I did with people my own age: most likely because I was dressed up in pretty much the same clothes. Thanks, Mum.

There was one old lady whom I particularly remember called Phyllis, who was a wonderful woman. She had married twice, but had no family left around her. She really took to Mum and me and kept telling us that she wanted to send me to Oxford when it became time for me to go to university. Can you imagine me at Oxford?

Whenever I used to stop by to say hello to Phyllis, she would always try to give me this envelope. We kept telling her that we couldn't accept it. In the end, Mum suggested that she give the envelope to a solicitor to keep safe.

Later, after she'd passed on, it turned out that it contained £96,000 worth of Guinness shares. Mum donated the money to a charity that Phyllis had supported for years, for which she had a great passion. It was in aid of white seals. I remember that I once gave Phyllis the biggest white seal cuddly toy I could find as a present; it was heart-warming to watch her face light up with pleasure.

The best thing about moving to Warbreck Hill Road was that my friends and I had a better place in which to play and hang out. We particularly enjoyed having girlie sleepovers. Gemma Rowland especially would stay over a lot. When the whole gang was round, there wasn't a lot of sleeping done, that's for sure – my mum had a nightmare trying to get us to settle down of a night. We all had such a good time together.

Aged nine, I still had dreams of dancing. Okay, so my horrible ballet teacher had kicked me out of class, but that didn't mean I suddenly stopped gyrating. Not even my old Lycra get-up could hold me back. No way! When the rhythm came and got me, I was lost in music.

As a mental fan of Michael Jackson, I used to try to recreate his dance routines. There I'd be in my bedroom, singing along to Jacko's hits with my very own red *Thriller*-style jacket that my nan had brought back from a trip to Vegas for me, my very own sequinned glove and my very own Michael-esque perm. At the time, I thought I looked the bee's knees. Of course, in reality, I looked more like Michael's pet monkey, Bubbles (I can't believe I can still remember his name).

No matter how heavy I got – and by nine, I was a right lard arse – I could still shake what my mamma gave me, which is more than you can say for some people half my size. But then some folks enjoy it and some don't: watching *Strictly Come Dancing* proves that. I was convinced that no matter what shape I was, I could show the world a thing or two when it came to strutting my stuff on the dance floor – and my mum, dad, nan and granddad were right behind me.

In 1988, Nan took me to the local Pontin's for a week. While there, I participated in its annual dance competition. A bunch of judges would pick so many kids out of each heat and then see the chosen few again at the final once the summer season was over.

In the first round, I danced to Michael Jackson's 'Bad'. An obvious choice of song, bearing in mind I simply loved the guy, but I had to make use of that perm somehow. I knew the music inside and out, and for the duration of the three-minute routine that I had practised so intently day after day back home, I was immersed in the beats and rhythms.

As I tossed my head around like a maniac and flung my arms out, I forgot all about the tens of people looking on. I felt so at home on the dance floor. I felt it was where I belonged, even though I was dripping with sweat and gasping for breath by the time I'd finished my surprisingly energetic routine. Without wanting to sound big-headed, I knew I had done well. I knew that I had impressed the judges.

Indeed, that day I won a silver-plated plaque, engraved with the slogan 'Disco-Dancing Winner'. I still have it to this day.

Speaking of awards, I recently won another that now sits alongside that disco-dancing trophy on my mantelpiece. Just before *Oliver!* opened in winter 2008, I had a call from my agent Gav, telling me that I had won the *TV Times* prize for Reality-TV Star of 2008. It was decided by public vote, so thank you for voting if you did. It was a real boost for me to receive the honour; and I have to say, it beats my Pontin's one hands down.

Back to Pontin's – and, of course, the final. The silver-plated plaque was awarded simply to mark my achievement in making it through to the next round: the major prize was still to be won.

The seminal event took place a few weeks later at the Pontin's in Morecambe. Not the most glamorous of places, I'm sure you'll agree, and even less so on the day. The rain was beating down and the wind was howling around the chalets, so it was a pretty typical late summer day in the British Isles.

Yet in spite of the miserable weather, I felt confident. I was sure I was a winner. How could I possibly lose? Which other kid would have a sequinned glove and moves like the ones I had been rehearsing for hours on end?

Sure, most of the other contestants looked like they had just pirouetted out of a ballet class with their lean limbs and heads held high in the air. But I knew I had something more: I had natural talent. I had the drive and determination to win. Yep, even at nine, I was a right little fighter.

Another thing that I thought stood me in good stead was my outfit, which my nan had pieced together herself. We reckoned it should have won an award in its own right. Now bear in mind, at the time this look was the height of fashion. I won't lie to you: it was garish. But this was Pontin's, it was a dance competition and I was a little girl.

My costume consisted of a shiny silver skirt that looked more like a wrap of tin foil around my waist, a white baggy top that had sequins on it, and a Wacko Jacko-style trilby that Nan had painstakingly customized with glitter – only by the time we had braved it through the wind and rain, my hat was looking rather less sparkly.

As I waited for my turn, I wasn't too impressed by the talent on show. Yeah, the girls and boys could throw a shape, but I knew that I could throw better ones. Shapes that didn't even have names.

Backstage, the rest of the kids around me were warming up or doing some last-minute practice. It was my first real competition, so it was all new to me. Nerves were building up in my tum (or was I just peckish?). Aside from the infamous 'oak tree' pantomime, I'd never performed in front of a crowd this size before. This was a whole new experience. Nevertheless, I was determined to enjoy myself.

As I zoned out, all I could hear were pushy mums yelling at their kids and saying stuff like, 'Don't let her watch your dance moves.' I was shocked. The mums didn't seem to care about their little ones' feelings. They just wanted them to win – and not so their kids could be proud of their own achievement, but so the mums could lord it over all the other parents, who would naturally be dealing with their sobbing progeny who had missed out on winning the prize.

I was lucky: Mum, Dad and my whole family were

supportive, yet they didn't care whether I won or not. I mean, of course they wanted me to do well so I'd be happy, but they really just wanted me to enjoy myself.

My family have never pushed me into doing anything I didn't want to. I was the one who wanted to dance and to sing, and they were always there behind me, rooting for me. If I won something or I excelled at something, they were the first ones to cheer me on and give me a big congratulatory hug. If something didn't work out the way I wanted it to, they were there to help me deal with it. They certainly never told me off for missing a move or singing out of tune.

All through my life, they have given me independence, and yet been there for me if I needed them. They taught me that the most important thing about a performance is to have a good time, and in doing so give people – the audience – an entertaining experience.

Throughout my career, that is what I have believed. Even when I appeared on *I'd Do Anything*, it was never about being famous. I love singing and I loved seeing the faces of the people looking back at me. If they were smiling, then I knew that I was doing something right.

Assessing the other kids in the Pontin's show, I felt relatively confident that I had this particular prize sewn up. Nonetheless, when my name was called, I felt as nervous as hell.

Stepping out in front of the audience was scarier than I'd anticipated; much more frightening than in the earlier heat. Even though the lights were only dimly lit over the crowd, I could still see them staring right back at me, scrutinizing my every move and no doubt thinking, 'Is she too fat to be a dancer?'

Fat or not, it was what I wanted to do and nothing was going to stop me. As the intro to Michael Jackson's 'Bad' filled the hall, I counted myself in and launched into my routine. As soon as I was lost in the music, my nerves totally disappeared. Swirling around the floor, I felt like Jacko himself, confident that every move I made was successful.

Although I was caught up in the eye of my very own dance storm, I could sense that the audience loved what I was doing. When my performance came to an end, I was reassured to discover that my intuition had been right – they were very much on my side.

Naturally, the first person I looked to as I took my bow was Nan. As the applause rang out in my ears, all I cared about was what she had thought. From the expression of elation on her face, she was as pleased as punch. She looked proud and I was so happy that I had made her feel that way.

I ran offstage into her arms and she hugged me warmly.

'You were fantastic, Jodie,' she told me as she squeezed me tightly. 'You were the best, mark my words.'

Checking out the rest of the show, I couldn't help but agree, as some of the contestants who followed in my wake were definitely nowhere near as good.

Then it was the turn of a girl whose name has rather conveniently been lost in the mists of time. Sporting an unsightly ball of curly hair and a ridiculous Lycra outfit that was trimmed with diamanté (though no more ridiculous than mine, looking back), Girl A strode to the centre of the stage and waited for her music to start. She looked fierce and, like I had done, she looked determined to win. She was the Dolph Lundgren to my Sly Stallone in *Rocky IV*. It was going to be a battle, that's for sure. I had to win. Win I would, I was convinced, because I knew that my routine was great. No girl with a globe of curls was going to whoop my ass (said the Jacko fan with the copycat perm).

When my nemesis's music sprang into life, Girl A was off, like a rabbit out of its trap, spinning around like a Lycra-clad whirlwind. The audience were certainly impressed, 'ooh'ing' and 'aah'ing' at the right bits. I'm not going to lie: I was absolutely fizzing. This girl was good and I didn't like it one bit. I had done the best I could – and I thought she was on a par with me.

Then, just as I thought that perhaps we were neck and neck in the competition, the clever little minx pulled a blinder out of the bag. She did the splits. One minute she was standing on two feet, the next her legs were telling the time and it was 6 o'clock. I'm not going to mince my words: I was more gutted than a turkey at Christmas.

Needless to say, her splits won her the title. I was a runner-up, however, so I couldn't complain. That went to show the teacher who'd chucked me out of dance class, eh? Who's busting some moves now?

While I might not have come away with the top prize, I definitely came away with a buzz for showbiz. I'd relished the dancing and the audience reaction. My nan told me that when I came offstage, I couldn't stop smiling. I just loved being in the spotlight – but I was most excited at the thought of having given an audience a good time.

That's something I've carried through my entire career. For me, it's not just about being a singer or an actress, it's about being an entertainer.

There was one aspect of performing that I secretly adored. It was that when I was dancing – when I was lost in music – I lost all sense of myself. Under those bright, unforgiving lights, ironically, I got to escape from being big.

9

School Days

As it turned out, Elmslie Girls' School was actually quite a nice place to attend. To start with, the school was run by Miss Smithies and Mrs Humpidge, who were a lot nicer than Mrs Flemming had ever been, even though they too ran a tight ship.

To me, Smithies and Humpidge seemed a lot fairer and a great deal more supportive than the old witch, so I had a greater respect for them. These were women whose plan was to raise a generation of girls who said 'please' and 'thank you': a grand ambition, and one that we tried to achieve.

As it was a Church of England school, the teachers were keen to bring a little godliness into our lives. Every morning, we'd gather in the school hall to say our prayers. Sometimes, we'd be asked to pray by ourselves, which meant the huge hall would fall silent while we all asked God to bring us as many sweets as possible, or begged for the school to burn down so we could get off by lunchtime.

Saying your prayers is a weird thing because you always feel a bit stupid while you're doing it. And when you're in assembly, with the whole school saying prayers in their heads, the silence can be very uncomfortable, because you are always worried that your stomach might make an unearthly noise or – worse still – that you'll let off a big fat juicy bottom burp and everyone will hear you do it.

Of course, that's exactly what happened to me one morning. Only, I came up with a cunning plan to avoid total embarrassment; or so I thought. As I stood there, deep in my own thoughts, I could feel a smelly gas building up 'downstairs'. I knew that its intensity was such that, within moments, I'd no longer have control of it and I would have to let rip. I was guessing it was going to be a smelly one.

'Can I risk letting one off here in the assembly hall in front of the rest of the kids?' I pondered. 'Can I stand them all pointing fingers at me?' No, I bloody couldn't. Being weighty and teased for it was enough to have to deal with for now; I didn't want to give everyone something else to rib me about.

So, in the middle of our silent prayer, I got up, excused myself loudly, stepped out of the hall ... and pretended to faint there and then. As I fell and caused a commotion, I managed to squeeze out my deadly ass gas without anyone noticing.

Well, I say that. While no one may have noticed the sound of my wet parp as I hit the deck, anyone with a nose who rushed to my aid would have known instantly that something had happened. Luckily, they spared my blushes by not making an issue of my iffy whiff.

As it turned out, my plan was successful on many levels. My teachers were so concerned by my fainting spell that they called my mum so she could take me home. Of course, as soon as Mum arrived and took one look at me, she knew in an instant that I'd pulled off a masterstroke of deception once again. I may have been able to fool my schoolteachers, but I sure as hell couldn't pull the wool over Mum's eyes.

That wasn't the only time I hoodwinked the staff. When I got my first period, aged eleven, I hated it, but as I moaned that I never wanted another one, my mum calmly wrote a note for the school to get me out of gym class. This was, I discovered, such a great tool with which to absent myself from Phys. Ed. that I used it every other week. Consequently, my teacher said she never knew a girl who had so many – but it was either that or go out in the freezing cold, wearing the short P.E. skirt that I dreaded wrapping round my wide hips, so I really didn't have much of a choice.

Life at Elmslie proved to be a lot more eventful than at Langdale. As I got older, I got a lot more competitive. I was always trying to do better than everyone else. I remember once when I took part in an egg-and-spoon race, I started shouting at my mate Emma Rathbone, who was beating me, 'Let me win, let me win!' She never did – and I've never got over it.

Sadly, I had to put up with people making fun of me and my size. There were a few nasty girls, including one who would pick on anyone if they were wearing too much eyeliner – this from a girl who must have taken a bath in fake tan. Yet every school has them.

One girl in particular tried to make my life at school a misery. She would tease me and push me and play the right bully. What she didn't know was that I had Supermum on my side, and after a bit of mummy magic, this girl was transformed into a new improved pupil. She came in the next day all smiles, and even shared her pencils with me. What a result.

Being heavy and picked on meant that I generally kept myself to myself at school. I wasn't anywhere near as confident as I am now and I was yet to discover that humour could be a great way of defending myself. That would come later, when my teachers would say in my reports: 'Jodie would do better if she wasn't such a joker in the class.'

I was an able student, but I wouldn't say I was a brainbox – though I would later gain A-star grades at GCSE without too much revision. I liked art and drawing, and music. In fact, I joined the school choir, which performed in assemblies and put on various concerts throughout the year. I have to confess that my reasons for joining weren't entirely driven by my passion for singing, but something rather more prosaic.

In assembly, all the students had to sit on the wooden floor of the hall – except for the choir, who were elevated above on chairs. My membership of the group made me much more comfortable during my school years, I have to say. In addition, of course, I also learned a lot about my voice and music in general.

My other favourite subject was English, probably because I liked to read so much. I wasn't your typical girl, though, losing myself in the stories of Enid Blyton. I preferred a good scare and devoured the Point Horror series of books, which told creepy tales of murderous boyfriends and vengeful gal pals that would have me on the edge of my seat as I turned each page.

These books also gave me an opportunity to use my entrepreneurial skills. Oh, I would have made Sir Alan Sugar proud. I used to get the books from my nan, who would bring them back for me from her trips to Las Vegas. As the titles were only available in America at the time, I reckoned I could make a few bob by renting them out at 5p a time. The scheme was a roaring success, only I didn't make that much money out of the enterprise because I wasn't all that great at collecting the dosh. But at least the thought was there.

Despite my *Apprentice*-like acumen, I knew that the high-flying business route wasn't one I wanted to take in life. Instead, I briefly considered the idea of becoming a vet. I love animals; my family home is like an animal refuge. So the job sounded heavenly to me. It would mean that I would be able to spend all my waking hours looking after creatures and nursing them back to health, just like Dr Doolittle.

Then it was pointed out to me that the job probably wouldn't be as much fun as I hoped – because I'd have to put the very poorly animals to sleep. I could never do that. Just the idea of looking at a sickly cat or dog lying on a table gazing up at me with its sorrowful eyes, while I held in my hand a big syringe full of some concoction that would kill it, made my stomach turn. There was no way I could ever do it, even if it was to take a poor little beast away from its pain. So that was that. Being a vet was scratched off my list of things to do.

Next, I fancied the idea of becoming a Disney animator. I was pretty good at art and drawing and adored the magic of Disney, so I reckoned that it might just be the right path to take. After all, it would mean that I'd still be working with animals of sorts: two-dimensional ones.

I was even more keen to do it when Mum and Dad took me to Disney World, Florida, where I got to see the animators at work. I was so impressed with their talents. I loved the idea of creating and drawing characters that would bring joy to so many people, and give them some of their happiest early memories that would last for the rest of their lives.

Once again, however, that career path petered out. Somewhere inside of me, I think I knew there was a natural performer waiting to burst out, however unlikely it might have seemed to those around me. I loved to sing and I loved to dance – was there any chance I could make a future out of that?

As I approached my teens, I took more of an interest in plays at Elmslie. They staged one or two a year, under the stewardship of a wonderful drama teacher called Mrs Carter, who was just as you'd imagine a performing-arts tutor to be. I was lucky in that I always got cast, usually in the comic roles. I thought of myself as a bit of a performing seal. I adored making people laugh, which probably explains all my practical jokes in class, when I'd flick ink about and just be cheeky in general. In all honesty, I think part of my motive in playing the fool was to provide a distraction from my looks; a defence of, 'I may be fat and look like a fella, but I'm funny!'

Unfortunately, due to my physical appearance – stocky and boyish – and the fact it was an all-girls' school, I was often cast in the male roles in the plays. So when we staged productions of *Les Misérables*, *The Mikado* and *HMS Pinafore*, I played blokes in them all. I even played the Phantom in *Phantom of the Opera*.

To this day, I'm surprised I never ended up a butch lesbian. Thank God for my mum dressing me up as a fifty-year-old; that kept me straight. Mind you, reviewing the pictures, I was like a mini Pat Butcher: a mini Pat Butcher with maxi love handles.

So – and you might well ask – how did I get to be so big? I mean, I was a good four or five stone heavier than most kids my age. To begin with, it wasn't that I ate all that badly; it was just that I ate a lot.

Don't blame Mum. She wasn't the kind of mother who gave me bad foods. We ate a mix of everything. Healthy stuff, like fruit and veg, and then I'd have the odd treat like a KFC or chips or a full fry-up. The thing was, I liked to eat. What kid doesn't, growing up? And I guess it's fair to say that I didn't just have a sweet tooth, I had a sweet gob.

When I headed off to Elmslie of a morning, I would take my little purse full of 'lunch' money – yet I wouldn't use it to buy a healthy dinner, but to purchase snacks. I would stuff my face with any old rubbish. Preferably any old rubbish that came covered in chocolate or tasted just dandy.

I couldn't help myself. I loved sweets. Why are they made to be so lip-smackingly yummy? For enjoyment, that's why. So while the other kids were buying a single mini swiss roll from the tuck shop, I was getting myself two Chomps and a KitKat.

As I got older, and moved into my teens, I discovered that I used food as a comfort. I became what you would call a 'secret feeder'. I never wanted my mum and dad to see me eat. They knew that I was unhappy about being heavy and that if I ate rubbish, I got upset.

The silly thing was that when I was upset, all I could do was turn to the snacks for comfort. That's the funny thing about food – it's always there for you. And for that split second, as the chocolate melted on my tongue, I'd feel so much better. It was only when I'd swallowed my snack that the regrets would flood into my mind and I'd get angry with myself. But that didn't stop me from repeating the pattern.

Some nights, I would creep out of bed and sneak into the kitchen. I'd covertly steal some biscuits, and then race back to my bedroom, where I would enjoy munching on my booty alone under the covers.

It was just like having an addiction: I needed a fix of sugary loveliness, but I didn't want people to know that I was 'shooting up' with a Cadbury's Creme Egg. I was ashamed of myself because I knew what I was doing. When I gorged, I felt bad about it – but I only felt that way for a brief moment. Then I'd go and eat more. When I looked in the mirror, I was never happy with what I saw: yet even my reflection was not enough to scare me out of my kamikaze eating habits.

I tried my best to hide the evidence, tucking wrappers under my bed or shoving them into my make-up box. God, I tell you, the back of my bed held more empty sweet wrappers than a raid at Charlie's Chocolate Factory. Throwing the packaging in the bin would have given me away immediately, you see, so I had to think of every trick in the book to conceal what I was up to.

Nevertheless – and wouldn't you know it? – I often ended up getting busted by Mum. You know what mothers are like: they can nose anything out. Those confrontations were awful. I'd lie, and say the wrappers weren't mine, that I hadn't eaten anything – even that it was the dogs that were to blame – but Mum saw right through me. Gently, she'd ask me why I'd done it, when I knew it only made me sad.

In response, I'd lash out at her horribly and say, accusingly, 'You're not thin yourself!' After which outburst, I'd feel even guiltier.

It was very tender ground for my mum to walk on, and frequently upsetting for her, because she could see how distraught I was. Meanwhile, her distress would make me feel wretched: what sort of a daughter was I to put my mum through this? I'd sense her disappointment in me.

And then, of course, I'd eat to make myself feel better. It was an unending, vicious circle that rotated, day after day.

10

Animal Quackers

Perhaps it was because I felt so low, and was sometimes picked on at school, that I found it easier to relate to animals than people. I would look after waifs and strays and they were never cruel to me. Maybe I even saw a bit of myself in them.

I'm not saying I was unloved or left to fend for myself; I was spoiled to death by my family. But deep down, knowing that I wasn't happy with the way I looked, I think I identified with animals that no one else wanted, because they didn't look right and they didn't belong either.

Over the years, my family has taken in loads of strays from the Easterleigh Animal Sanctuary. In fact, you could say that the Prenger household has been a bit of a Noah's Ark. We've had a rabbit with one ear, whom we called Pardon; a rabbit that was blind in one eye, called Blinker; and we had three chickens named Kentucky, Fried and Chicken, who had their own ranch in the garden with a sand pit.

Now, these weren't just any chickens, let me tell you. They were fancy little blighters, with big furry heads, which required classical music to help them lay eggs. When Kentucky went to that great big chicken coop in the sky – he was the one we referred to as One-Eyed Cock, because he only had one eye – we gave him a state funeral on a par with Gandhi's. But then that's *chez* Prenger for you: it's a whole other world.

When we lived at the hotel, we never had as many pets as we do now. Jules was our very first pet. He was an apricot poodle who had been badly treated. Then we got Pepsi and Chase. Chase was a lovely, friendly dog and my granddad fell in love with him. You can imagine how heartbreaking it was when Chase passed on, at only nine years old – Granddad was just devastated and locked himself away for a week.

Pepsi and Chase used to have a third playmate, a white poodle called Chico, but he was an absolute mentalist who hated me. He despised me to my very bones, which was weird, because I adore animals and in most cases they love me too.

This was back when I was a baby. Mum and Dad first knew something was not right with Chico when he went for me. My mum was frantic, knowing how dangerous a dog can be with a little 'un. I was about eighteen months old. Chico suffered from very random mood swings, and one day he became incredibly fierce and just raced across the room towards me. Luckily, both Mum and Dad were with me at the time and thank God they were: it took the two of them to hold me and hold Chico off.

The vet later told Mum that Chico was too closely bred, which was why he wasn't easy to deal with. So my grandparents looked after him, but even they found him hard going.

My poor granddad was the one who had to try and keep him calm. Granddad used to hypnotize him with a song, which did the trick. Now, by 'song', I mean he sang something like, 'Dee lii dee lii diddly deee' – hey, try it if you too have a wild dog; you never know, it might help. Every time Chico went a bit crazy, Gramps would sing and everything would be all right again. For a while, the vet prescribed the dog equivalent of Valium, too, but it just made Chico like a zombie, and it wasn't fair. In the end, my folks had to take the hard decision to have him put down.

When I was a bit older, I experienced another loss when my prized bright yellow budgie went missing. Dolly was her name and I loved that bird with all my heart. Sometimes, I'd sit for hours and just watch her flapping her gorgeous golden wings in the cage.

Then, when I was about nine or ten, my world fell apart around me. Bouncing into the living room one morning to say hi to Dolly, I was horrified to see her cage was empty and its door wide open. It seemed that my darling brother Marko, then a toddler, had unintentionally freed Dolly – although my parents didn't tell me that at the time, of course. Understandably, they had no desire to start World War Three in their own home.

After a frantic search of the house, I discovered that my little birdie was nowhere to be found. She had flown away.

I couldn't bear life without Dolly. Just like that, she was gone and I was left with an empty cage. To say I burst into tears is an understatement. I cried like I had never cried before. How could I go on without my favourite budgie by my side?

My parents didn't know how to begin to console me. After they had made a thorough search of the immediate area, Mum and Dad did what all good parents would do. They hit the streets of Blackpool to locate Dolly.

Well, when I say Dolly, what they were really doing – unbeknownst to me – was trying to find Dolly Mark Two. Yep, soon after they had given up any hope of finding my pride and joy, Mum and Dad had decided that they needed a Plan B. That plan was to search every pet shop in Blackpool for a bird that looked exactly the same as my missing Dolly.

When I got home from school, I was overjoyed to hear the chirp of a dandy bird. Dolly was back! I rushed into the room and there she was: my bright yellow budgie tweeting away as happily as ever. I was over the moon to have my little friend back.

Of course, I didn't realize that this bird was an imposter. When you're young, you take things for granted. My parents were simply relieved that they had managed to fool me into believing that Dolly was home, as it meant all my tears dried up and there was a big fat smile on my big fat face.

Sadly, as you'll see time and time again, the life of Jodie rarely runs smoothly. The very next day, I bounded downstairs to bid my budgie a good morning and was stunned, then devastated, to discover Dolly lying dead in the bottom of her cage. Tears flowed freely again and Mum could only look to Dad, knowing that they had wasted a grand total of fourteen quid on a budgie that had lasted less than twenty-four hours in the Prenger madhouse of fun.

As far as I knew, though, this Dolly was the Dolly I had loved for ages. Naturally, we had to give her a send-off we knew she'd be proud of. We buried her in the garden, and I even painted her a gravestone.

Today, our house is jammed to the gills with all manner of animals. As I'm now living in London, I miss them all dearly. If I could, I'd have a chicken or two down here with me in my apartment, but something tells me that having a chicken roaming around a London flat is not quite the done thing.

If you walked past our Blackpool house, you'd swear it was a zoo. We have a Yorkshire terrier called Louis, who was given to us by Lorraine who makes our curtains. When he was born, he looked like a cross between a Rottweiler and a poo. He's the most spoilt pup ever: if he doesn't get his Marks & Spencer beef, he gets mardy. Sometimes, I'll nip off and get him a Happy Meal from McDonald's. I feel like a really bad mum now I've just confessed that.

We also have a second Yorkshire terrier called Gizmo – he's my Yorkshire terrorist. He's the latest addition from Easterleigh. We'd only gone to pick up a new rabbit, but came home with him, too. It took him some time to settle in; he'd leave little messages all around the house, but he's such a cutie that you can't be angry with him for long. He hates men, which has come in handy when I've brought home some deadbeat boyfriends. He can always spot 'em, even if I can't.

Rounding out the family are our two thirteen-year-old Lhasa apsos, Honey and Arnie. A few years ago, Arnie scared the life out of me when he had an epileptic fit. Luckily, Mum was on hand to stick her finger in his mouth to make sure he didn't swallow his tongue. Believe it or not, poor mum ended up with blood poisoning as a result and had to go to hospital for a transfusion.

I could go on all day about our brood, but I won't. I'll just give a final mention to our three rabbits, four tortoises, two budgies, one cockatiel, two parrots, and the fish in the pond. Phew!

As you can probably tell from all that, I'm mad soft with animals. I can't even watch films like *King Kong* or *Free Willy* because I can't bear to see animals in pain. If there's a scene where a dog so much as twists its foot, I can't watch it or I'm in floods of tears. Movies like *Kung Fu Panda* are the only option because I know there'll be a happy ending. Now, I know what you're thinking: how sad can she be? But show me *Bambi* and it just kills me.

Throughout my life, if I've ever spotted an animal that looks unhappy, I'm the first person to help it. For example, there was a lost dog that I rescued when I was around twenty. My mum was driving through Blackpool and saw this girl heaving a huge black-and-white dog along the streets.

'God, that poor girl is really struggling with that dog,' she thought to herself – never thinking in the world that it might actually be me.

Of course, it was. My mum's face was a picture when I turned up at the house with the very same dog in my arms. That particular pup had a tag on his collar, so once I'd managed to drag him home, we called the owners and they came and got him. Apparently, he kept jumping over their fence and getting out on his own, so they were pleased to have tracked him down.

There was another occasion, when I was about twenty-two,

when I was strolling home and came across this sorrowful-looking black-and-white spaniel. He was sitting, seemingly lost and lonely, on the street corner. Simply staring into his face and seeing the whites of his eyes was enough to make me decide that I was there to save the day.

I called my parents and told them that I'd found an abandoned dog. I wanted to wrap him up in towels and try to nurse him back to health – could they come to help?

My mum asked me where I'd found the dog, and then suggested that we went to see if any of the neighbours knew where he had come from. I wanted to argue that the dog had no home and that I had rescued him from a life of misery on the Blackpool streets. But Mum reasoned with me that if he was actually someone's and I'd 'rescued' him, they might be as broken-hearted as I would be if I lost my dog.

So Mum and Dad came to find me, and then went from door to door in the neighbourhood, trying to ascertain whether or not a dog was missing. I remember sitting in the car just praying that no one would lay claim to the mutt, so that I could take him back home and pamper him.

Yet when Mum and Dad came to a house on the corner and asked the person who lived there if they were missing a dog, the answer was not the one I wanted to hear. Mum had found the dog's home. His owner said that the spaniel was so friendly that he would just go off with anyone. I was gutted. Yet, deep down, I knew the dog would be happy being with his family. And if it had been the other way around and I'd lost my dog, I'd want a good soul to return it to me too.

Animals really have been there for me all my life. I love them to bits. In truth, it was just as well that I found some affection from them – because as I was growing up, I discovered that it was rather less than forthcoming from other quarters.

11

Boys, Boys, Boys

As I was larger than most girls, and didn't look anything like a catwalk model, boys never bothered too much with me as I grew up. Whether it was because I was so heavy, or because with my short hair and baggy outfits I actually looked like a boy, I could never work out. But they gave me a wide berth, that's for sure.

Nevertheless, I thought about them, even though I never had any of them sniffing around me. Actually, that's not entirely true. When I was younger, I did have a boyfriend. Yes, a real-life boyfriend. Okay, so I was four years old and it lasted about five minutes, but it was still a boy and I got a kiss out of it. Whether or not he truly liked me is another matter. But as I've come to realize, you can never really work guys out half the time, whether they're four or forty.

His name was Christopher Musto ... and in all honesty, I can't remember too much beyond that. All I can recall is that we were playing kiss chase one day, and after that we agreed to be boyfriend and girlfriend.

Three days later, I was picking up the pieces of my broken heart when the romance came to a sudden end. I don't know why it did. Maybe we just didn't see a future in it. Or more likely for kids of our age, we were too busy watching the latest episodes of *He-Man* and *She-Ra*. Who could compete with that?

While Christopher might have been my first-ever boyfriend (of three whole days, let's not forget), my first kiss came a year earlier. That's right, when I was three years old. Naturally, it was just an innocent peck on the lips; I'm not some freak from *The Jeremy Kyle Show*.

My suitor's name was Steve Brown and he was the son of my mum's mate Joan. She was getting married for the second time at our hotel. At the party, Joan told Steve to give me a kiss, which he did. In truth, I can't recall what it was like. But Steve, if you're reading this, don't be offended. We were so young, I'd be unlikely to remember even the best kiss in the world. Mum later told me that she and Joan had always hoped that Steve and I might get it together one day. Sadly for them, we never did.

Fast forward a few years, and I started to find older men attractive. Top of my wish list were those dandy fellas from Take That; Mark Owen in particular. Back then, most girls fancied him. He was just so cute and sweet and sensitive. And he sang so beautifully. I remember when I heard Take That's 1993 Christmas single 'Babe' for the first time, my tummy had butterflies in it and I memorized the words immediately.

As far as I was concerned, Mark was the perfect man. Sometimes I used to dream that if he ever came to Blackpool, I'd walk into him and fall over so that I could be rushed to hospital, where he'd come to visit, fall in love with me and then we'd end up getting married. Jodie Owen does have a ring to it, doesn't it?

Funnily enough, when I was appearing in *I'd Do Anything*, I got to meet one of Take That. Sadly, it wasn't little Marky. It was Gary Barlow, who actually looked pretty hunky. He'd come to watch the show with his gorgeous kids and wife and had asked a runner if I would come and meet them all after the programme, because his kids really liked me.

Can you believe it? Take That star Gary Barlow wanted to meet with me, Jodie Christine Prenger ... well, his kids did. They are totally adorable, I have to say. I ended up being more captivated by them than I did by Gary.

It was an unbelievable situation in many ways. It was so surreal that I had to keep pinching myself. Luckily, I managed to hold it together during our brief meeting, without reverting back to being a kid and making a fool of myself. Fifteen years earlier, I would have been a sobbing mess, no doubt clinging to his thigh for dear life. Thankfully, age had done me wonders and given me the maturity to handle myself properly.

Gary is a lovely man – more handsome now than he was back in the day, in my opinion. He is charming and funny and very charismatic. Call me fickle, but I'm a sucker for a handsome guy.

As a teenager, I was always on the lookout for that someone special, forever prepared to fall head over heels. The trouble was, it felt like lads were looking out for me too – and then running as fast as they could in the opposite direction. Boys and I just didn't go together. As I've explained, I wasn't exactly what you'd call the prettiest of girls. With more chins than a Chinese phone book, a dodgy, cropped perm and massive specs that covered half my face, I suspected it was sometimes hard to tell if I was male or female anyway.

As I hit puberty, I began to form 'lady curves' – but you had to look really closely to see them. Unfortunately for me, those telltale contours were being totally swamped by my all-round curviness: the latter caused by my weight rather than my gender. I was pretty shapeless at this point. Well, 'ball-like' perhaps might be the best way of putting it.

I certainly wasn't what you'd call a svelte girl, which ultimately meant that no boy was interested in me at all. Not one. For years, I had to make do with fancying guys from afar – and put up with them walking straight past me into the arms of a skinnier, prettier alternative.

I spent my adolescence, hormones ablaze, listening to my mates telling me about who they had snogged at the local ice-skating rink. All I could do was nod and mutter, 'Oh, you never did,' and that was that. Then I'd go home and dream about Mark Owen or something, and wish that one day I could have a boyfriend too. How sad.

I can't recall now if I ever reached a conclusion as to whether it was wholly my looks that stopped me from getting lucky with boys, or if the fact that I attended an all-girls' school was also a factor. With so little practice, just talking to a fella would turn me to jelly. When you're trapped in a big body, you can sometimes forget how people see you – yet the look in boys' eyes as I tried to muster the courage to say 'hi' reminded me all too well.

While I wasn't happy about my weight, I never let it get me really down – at least, not that I used to show people. Although there were no boyfriends on the current horizon, I was optimistic enough to believe that one day my Mr Right would ride along on his stallion and sweep me off my feet.

Consequently, you can imagine my excitement when I discovered that someone fancied me. Yes, someone actually wanted to go out with *me*.

It all started one afternoon when I was about thirteen. Some of my school pals and I went to the local fair for a few hours of fun and frolics. While we were wandering aimlessly through the fairground, talking about boys and what we'd watched on the telly the night before, we copped an eyeful of this guy working on one of the rides, whom we all reckoned was a bit of a looker. He was older than us and he looked really fit in his T-shirt and jeans. He was the kind of mysterious older guy for whom heroines in Judy Blume books went weak at the knees.

Bearing in mind I was like a desert with not so much as one camel setting foot anywhere near me, I was ready to fall in love with a lamp post. Now that this guy had come into my world – albeit from a distance and without him knowing anything about it – I could fantasise about a real-life boy. It didn't matter to me if he was aware I existed ... and, let's face it, he clearly wasn't.

We must have looked like a right bunch of idiots, standing there just staring and pointing at this guy. I can't remember if anyone actually spoke to him; I doubt they did, as even the more confident girls in the group would have stopped short of going over and talking to him. We were all mouth and that was pretty much it. Funnily enough, if we saw him now, I bet we'd not even give him a second look. It's odd what appeals to you at that age.

A week or so later, it was Valentine's Day, a date that I normally let pass me by. After all, for me it was just like any other day: I'd wake up, go to school, come home and watch the telly. Well, if I'm honest, I suppose it did always feel a little bit different to most other days. In spite of myself, I couldn't help wondering if a secret admirer might declare his undying love for me. So far, no one had. But every year I was hopeful, if a little sceptical.

On this particular 14 February, I was in for a surprise – in more ways than one. There I was, mooching through the day, minding my own business, catching snatches of conversations between the girls at school about how many Valentine's cards they'd received, and generally feeling a bit forlorn.

When I got home, I found a note waiting for me. Of course, as I had never ever had any kind of Valentine's message before, I wasn't particularly excited about it, as I expected it to be nothing more than a charity card from my family. But when I opened the letter and skimmed through it, I had to catch my breath. It was a love note. Moreover, it looked like it was from the boy we had been checking out at the fair.

I knew that much, because in the letter he said that he had

seen us looking at him. Better still, he wrote that of all the girls he saw, he thought that I was the prettiest and that he wanted to get to know me better. He would like to meet up in town next week. Oh. My. God.

I read the letter again. Had I misinterpreted it? Had I walked into the wrong house? Had he confused me for one of the other girls? Why would he go for a fat bird like me? So many questions, but I didn't really care about the answers because a boy fancied me.

I immediately ran off to tell my mum, who humoured me and murmured in response, 'That's nice.' I couldn't wait to see the guy and actually talk to him.

Then nerves – and more questions – shot through my body. How could I speak to this boy? What did I have to say to him? He was way out of my league. If he were interested in me now, then he sure as hell wouldn't be once he'd heard what I had to say for myself. (Erm, nothing.)

And if I did go and meet him, what would I wear? I couldn't simply slip on my canary yellow jumpsuit or any of the eye-watering sparkly tops my mum had bought me. Maybe he was a Michael Jackson fan like me and I could impress him with my sequinned glove and *Thriller* jacket ... or maybe not.

I called my mates and told them the news. They couldn't believe it, but reassured me that I was one lucky girl. Oh, and I was. After all this time of being a social leper, a guy – and a relatively fit one at that – had finally shown some interest.

When it came to meeting him, I ditched the glitz and opted for a sensible top and trousers. Arriving at the rendezvous point, I was nervous and excited all at the same time. A lot was riding on this date. This could be the start of a whole new life for me. This could be the day that Jodie Prenger would land her first bona fide boyfriend.

And so I stood there, waiting – for five, ten, fifteen minutes. There was no sign of Fair Boy. Yet I was willing to give him some time. I tried to imagine what boys were like before a date: they must be so vain. He was probably fixing his hair and making sure he looked his best, so that he could bravely sweep me off my feet and romance me.

Twenty minutes passed. Maybe my watch was slow. Or maybe I had the wrong day. But they were just excuses. I knew, deep down, that I was fooling myself. The boy wasn't coming. He had obviously chickened out. Or worse: perhaps he had actually shown up, seen me, and scarpered pretty quickly. Whatever the reason, I stood there for almost half an hour, looking like a right idiot.

It later emerged that the boy hadn't stood me up. In fact, he had never even sent me the note. He really didn't know I existed. My so-called mates had decided it would be funny to make me think he was interested. How cruel is that?

The most stupid thing is that I fell for their trick, hook, line and sinker. How dumb am I? Why did I think this dreamboat would even consider meeting me? Me, who looked like some kind of Weeble. Except this Weeble did fall down and didn't bounce back up.

I was devastated. I really had a go at them for being so mean. They said they did it as a joke and that no harm was meant. Yet I couldn't help but feel so very hurt. These were my friends. I trusted them to be honest with me, and now I felt betrayed. I would never have dreamed of doing something like that to one of them, so why did they do it to me? That's what I couldn't fathom.

Don't get me wrong, I'm all for practical jokes – even extreme ones, like shaving off an eyebrow, for example – but to play with someone's emotions like that and to build someone up, only to pull the rug out from beneath them ... well, it was too much to bear.

My mum was brilliant, as usual. She told me that one day I would find a good man. She also reassured me that my mates probably weren't being intentionally cruel; that it was simply a poor joke that got out of hand. Eventually, I did forgive them.

Unfortunately, that wasn't the only time I was made to seem a fool in my teenage years. When one of the girls at school threw a fancy-dress party, I ended up looking like a right plonker.

I decided early on that I would go as Dracula. I can't remember exactly why I chose the infamous bloodsucker; I think I thought it would be fun to dress up and give people a scare. Also, I would get to wear a baggy shirt and a big black cloak, which would do me the world of favours by hiding my bulky frame.

Mum spent ages putting together the outfit for me, adding her own finishing touches. We dedicated hours to the makeover itself, slicking my hair away from my face, applying the white make-up and dabbing some fake blood across my mouth.

When Mum had completed the transformation, I checked myself out in the mirror (as even with Mum's legendary skills, the lack-of-reflection aspect of vampire lore wasn't part of my disguise). I looked brilliant. Mum agreed, and Dad and my grandparents said I looked like the best bloodsucking creature of the night that had ever stalked the earth.

The party was only at the end of our road, but Mum and Dad insisted on dropping me off. When I billowed out of the car in my black cloak, I was chuffed to bits with my appearance. My mum had done me proud with my costume. I just knew that the minute I walked in, everyone would stop and stare and say, 'Wow! You look amazing.'

Taking a deep breath, I pushed open the door to join the rowdy crowd. As soon as I'd stepped into the room, I went cold and I could feel the colour drain from my face (not that you could see that under two inches of white make-up and fake blood).

All of the guests were dressed in normal clothes. Not one person was in fancy dress. Not one. Not even the girl who was hosting. I was the only one standing there looking like I was dressed up for Halloween. It was exactly like that scene in *Bridget Jones's Diary*, when Renée Zellweger turns up at that party in her bunny-girl outfit.

Everyone froze, and then stared at me like I had two heads or something. I'm sure that the music might even have stopped. It was like a Western – all of them just standing there with their mouths open. I ran over to the host, who was looking at me like I was some kind of joke.

'Why is no one else dressed up?' I asked.

Looking me up and down like I was a piece of dirt on her shoe, she replied, 'Didn't you get my message? I changed my mind about making it fancy dress.'

Did she heck as like. She hadn't mentioned it to me once and she had had ample opportunity to do so at school. Had she done it on purpose so that I'd be a laughing stock? I wasn't sure, but I was furious.

As the group's guffaws rang in my ears, I chuckled along too. What other choice did I have? A few pals and I went upstairs to the bathroom and I wiped off the make-up that my mum and I had so carefully applied. As I did so, I couldn't help but wonder when I would have someone who would always be on my side, no matter what. When would I meet Mr Right?

12

The One That Got Away

Love is a many-splendoured thing. Love changes everything. All you need is love. Love hurts. And when you're thirteen, fools fall head over heels in love.

Having just about recovered from my very own Valentine's Day massacre, I thought perhaps I'd never find anyone to fall in love with again. But then … Gavin walked into my life. Well, actually, if I tell the story right, I walked into his.

Mum and I were out shopping one day, when we popped into Discount Wallpaper in Blackpool to have a look at a few of the designs (we were in the process of revamping my boudoir once again). We must only have been at the counter for three seconds before the young guy who worked there appeared from nowhere. No sooner had I looked up at him than I was in love. I swear, I could hear birds singing gaily in the trees and see love hearts forming around his face.

Now, let me describe Gavin for those of you not lucky enough to have laid eyes on him. He was gorgeous. He really was. Older than me, at around seventeen, he was tall and had dark hair. In a way, he had the look of a young Elvis Presley, whom I also adored. Without a doubt, Gavin was the best thing since sliced bread – and you know how I feel about food.

All I could do was stare. And stare is what I did, taking in every aspect of him, my mouth practically hanging open, so that when I was alone at night, I could recall everything about him. I didn't speak to him the next time we went to the shop or even the time after that. In fact, we went there so many times at my request, and Mum had to buy so many rolls of wallpaper as a result, that he must have thought we lived in a mansion.

When I heard his name for the first time, my knees nearly gave way and I had to reach for a nearby display of wallpaper to make sure I didn't hit the deck. Okay, so 'Gavin' might not be the sexiest name in the world, but to a thirteen-year-old girl without much boy action in her life, it was nothing less than sublime. I felt all gooey inside.

As time went on, my parents became friends with his parents, and I began to see a lot of Gavin. Of course, I never told him about my intense feelings for him, but he would have had to be blind not to notice. Whenever I saw him, my eyes would light up and my cheeks would turn a little rosy. I was as smitten as a kitten in mittens.

We were only ever friends, yet to some degree, that was okay with me: he wasn't going to go out with me, but at least we could hang out together. Clearly, in an ideal world, I would have wanted Gavin to walk into my school like Richard Gere in *An Officer and a Gentleman*, scoop me up in his arms and whisk me off to a world of romance, but that was never going to happen. Even I knew that. The scooping-me-up part would have been too difficult in itself.

Although I would have been mortified if Gavin himself had ever broached with me the subject of my crazed infatuation, everyone else in the world seemed to know about it. It was like I was wearing an 'I Love Gavin' T-shirt. It was just shining out of me for everyone to see. My mates knew, my mum and dad knew, my kid brother knew and Gavin's mum Carolyn did too. Talk about super cringe.

I blame my mum for the latter finding out, for Carolyn may only have suspected my feelings for her drop-dead gorgeous son before she popped round to our house one time, but my mum had more than confirmed them by the time she left.

As you already know, every year Mum would give my bedroom a makeover, and not just a lick of paint or a colour-scheme change. She'd go to town on giving the room its own special theme. This particular year – the year I was fourteen – I had asked my mother to base her makeover on the great stars of the past, such as Marilyn Monroe, Elvis Presley and Marlon Brando.

While I was out one day, she set to work creating the most amazing room I had ever seen. When I clapped eyes on it, I was astounded. Along one wall were giant murals of the three stars. They looked so life-like, it was incredible.

Upon closer examination, I noticed that on the Marlon Brando figure, Mum hadn't painted the actor's face. Instead, it was a face that was somehow familiar. When I studied it in depth, I gasped a little bit. It was Gavin. Gavin's face was right there on my wall. Looking at him staring down at me, it was like seeing the face of God staring back at me. You know, just like those people who think they've seen the face of Jesus or Mary in a potato or a pizza topping. I didn't know what to say to Mum. It was the single greatest thing I had ever seen!

Mum could tell that I was as happy as Larry. For the next few days, I would lie on my bed and just gaze at Gavin's face looking down at me. I'd while away hours in my room, daydreaming about him and imagining what it would be like to be his girlfriend. I was well and truly head over heels in love.

Sometimes, I'd even whisper sweet nothings into his painted ear. I'd say all the things I longed to say to him in real life, like: 'Gavin, I love you. Gavin, I want to be with you. Gavin, I want to marry you one day and have your children.'

On occasion – God, I'm so embarrassed to admit this – I'd even kiss Gavin's likeness and imagine that it was the real

Gavin I was snogging. Well, a girl can dream, can't she? And it beats practising on your hand ... oh, come on, we've all tried it. Sometimes that's all we have opportunity to do.

One day, Mum invited Carolyn round for a catch-up. During her visit, she took her through to my bedroom to show off her handiwork. At first, Carolyn didn't notice a thing and simply gave Mum a pat on the back for her artistic skills. But then – and I could see it in her face – it dawned on her that Marlon Brando looked a little more familiar than he should have.

'That's our Gavin,' she squealed, before dissolving into a fit of giggles. 'Oh, Jodie, you must love that.'

Carolyn and my mum started laughing heartily amongst themselves. But this was no laughing matter to me. I was red hot with anger. How could Mum have embarrassed me like that in front of Gavin's mum? Now Carolyn knew that I was in love with her son. (It never really dawned on me at the time that she might already have known.) Surely it was only a matter of hours before she'd tell him? After the truth was out, how would I be able to look him in the eye? He'd never want to speak to me – or even see me – if he thought I was lusting after him. What had Mum done? Had she ruined everything between us? I look back now and the expression 'mountain out of a molehill' springs to mind.

As it turned out, Mum hadn't ruined anything – probably because there was nothing there to destroy. As far as Gavin was concerned, I was just chubby Jodie who had a crush on him. It didn't stop him from liking me. In fact, I bet in some ways he probably even enjoyed the fact that someone out there, however fat she might have been, had the hots for him.

It took ages before I managed to come to terms with the fact that Gavin and I were never going to be anything more than friends, but that was fine. He was a good mate and that was a great thing to have. Of course, being a teenager, I still fancied the pants off him and whenever I saw him, I still felt all a-quiver. And good on Gav: he played the game well and played up to my infatuation.

For instance, there was a time when I became obsessed with a picture of David Beckham wearing a cream suit. For some reason, I thought it was the sexiest get-up I had ever seen and went on and on about how lovely I thought it looked. So the next time Gavin saw me, what did he do? Yep, strolled in wearing a cream suit of his very own. I was so overcome with joy, all I could do was hide in the toilet, too nervous and tongue-tied to utter a word to him. What an idiot I was.

As you have probably worked out already, making a fool of myself was a bit of a recurring theme as far as Gavin went. One night, my family and I were invited round to Gavin's parents' house for a strawberry fair, a charity event where they serve up strawberries and champagne.

All excited about seeing Gav, I'd gone out and bought myself a new outfit. Now bearing in mind that I was a hefty girl, I could only find clothes to fit me at Evans, which is by no means the coolest of shops for a girl of fifteen. But it was either go there or ask Billy Smart if I could borrow one of his big tops, so I'd opted for this stripy dress I'd found, which I thought looked all right on me. Of course, 'all right' back then meant all right when compared with a potato sack, or a grubby bedspread.

Feeling fairly confident in my new attire, I rolled up to the party with a massive smile on my face, thrilled to have the chance to hang out with Gavin. Unfortunately, that grin was wiped straight off my chops when I caught sight of a large older woman wearing the exact same dress. I was mortified. No teenager wants to be seen wearing the same clothes as an old biddy – and it's even worse when that old girl is standing just across a garden from you.

It was at that point that I realized that the stripes made

us look like deckchairs. All I can remember is thinking to myself, 'Please, lady, don't come any closer or we'll end up making a sofa.'

If that wasn't bad enough, later that same year there was another time when I was left with egg on my face. I'll never forget this. Gavin's sister Shelley had announced that she was planning to leave Blackpool to go and work on the cruise ships, so our parents and friends all got together to arrange a nautically themed farewell knees-up for her. All the lads were going to dress up as female sailors, wearing tiny knickers under their skirts that would spell out 'Goodbye Shelley' when they stood in a line.

It was a fantastic period of time, as everyone in the area was pitching in and there was a fabulous camaraderie among us. Most importantly, of course, it meant that I got to see a lot more of Gavin.

For my outfit at this extravaganza, I was planning to dress up like the Little Mermaid, even though 'little' was a word that I knew could never be thrown in my direction. My costume featured a fish tail, which meant that I wouldn't be able to walk about during the singsong we had planned. Therefore, it was decided that I would recline elegantly on a lounger instead.

When it came to the celebration, all seemed to be going well … until I plonked myself on said lounger. No sooner had my fat fins hit the canvas, I crashed through and ended up rolling around on my back – a bit like a fish out of water, as it goes – right there in front of Gavin.

Needless to say, the whole party thought the sight of Jodie breaking the furniture was absolutely hilarious and they all erupted into laughter, Gavin included. I was mortified, but by this stage in my life, I had decided to make light of things like that, rather than wallowing in misery about them, so I joined in with the general mirth.

I always say that people come into your life for a reason,

a season or a lifetime. I maintain to this day that the reason my sad schoolgirl crush on Gav happened was so that the Prengers got to meet and become the best of friends with Carolyn and Dave, his mum and dad; with his Aunty Pam; his sis Shelley; his brother Scott ... in fact, the whole family. I always loved his gran, Lucy – what a lady, very sadly missed – while his granddad Harold is in my mum and dad's rest home at the moment.

They truly are such glorious people, all with hearts of gold – and you don't get friends like that twice in a lifetime.

As for Gavin? Well, he's living happily ever after with a beautiful wife called Philippa and two lovely kids. I may not be in love with him any more, but I'm glad we both found our own fairy-tale endings, after all.

13

Jodie Finally Gets a Snog

When I was sixteen, I opted to study a BTEC in performing arts at the Fylde College in Blackpool. I could have stayed on at Elmslie and taken a drama course there, but I felt I'd been a goldfish in a bowl long enough – I needed to be a goldfish in a paddling pool at the very least.

The choice of subject was a no-brainer for me. Not only had I always loved singing and dancing, but, recently, I'd also received a wicked endorsement of my talents from people 'in the know'. My Elmslie drama teacher, Mrs Carter, had put me forward to audition for the National Youth Theatre. She was a complete star about it, and really helped me prepare for the testing experience.

Against all my expectations, I was successful. I spent three weeks working with the NYT, having workshops and progressing our ideas into a final performance. Bizarrely enough, Beth Winslet, Kate Winslet's sister, was in my group. She seemed to think she was amazing because she could cry at the drop of a hat. I just thought to myself, 'Yeah, love, if I stamped on your toe, then you really would wail.'

What a place Fylde was. It was there that I felt I finally got to do something with my theatre skills and develop my taste for showbiz. For a start, it was a mixed-gender institution, so I was freed from playing male roles at last. It also gave me my first opportunity to 'tread the boards' on a professional stage, as every year the college put on a musical at the Grand Theatre in Blackpool, a Grade II-listed venue that has the most gorgeous architecture, with a stunning dome atop its facade. It really is a beautiful building.

My favourite show there, without a doubt, has to be *The Hot Mikado*. Have you ever heard of *The Mikado*, a light opera by Gilbert and Sullivan? Well, this ran along the same lines, but the score included big show tunes with a gospel feel. I adore gospel music as it is, and to play the part of Katisha – one of the leads – and stand on a proper stage and sing my little heart out ... Well, that was when I knew I was doing what I really loved.

My college days also saw me discover nightclubbing with a passion. By the time I got to sixteen, I was practically gagging to get out on the streets of Blackpool and go on the rampage. I had my sights set on any man who would give me a second look.

My first night out was with some of the staff from my parents' rest home. It was my initiation into being on the razzle, so it was a whole new way of life for me. As it turns out, I'm not a big boozer. A couple of drinks and I'm tipsy. Mum says that makes me a cheap night out, which I was – but not in that way!

What I recall from that evening isn't much, but I do remember that I had a massive perm – my mum had curled my hair before I went out – and that I shepherded the woozy staff home. I might only have been sixteen, but I ended up the most sober, having to look after people who perhaps should have known better.

I didn't mind one bit. I'd been out on the town and I'd adored it. It soon became a regular pastime. Although the clubs were for over-eighteens, my tight perm and styling made me seem so old that it actually looked like I was chaperoning my mates. The best thing was, even though I was often self-conscious about my weight, in the darkened clubs I was able to let go and have a good time.

I liked dancing to the chart tunes at the clubs like Main Street. I loved to people-watch and, of course, check out boys from afar. Frustratingly, just like at the ice rink, that's all I could do because none of the boys ever dared to look at me, in case they caught my eye and I spent the rest of the night hunting them down.

Although I usually laughed off the fact that I didn't have a boyfriend, it did start to get to me. I was a sixteen-year-old girl. All my mates were copping off with blokes and there was me holding their blimmin' coats. It wasn't fair. There was many a night when I'd lie in my bed sobbing away, wondering why I was the only one left on the shelf. A shelf that was straining under my fat arse. I knew I was a big girl, but I was blossoming in what some might say was a pretty – if beefy – way.

It didn't help that Mum would always curl my hair into the tightest ringlets before I went out … it makes me think now, was that her crafty way of keeping boys away from me? I mean, sometimes my hair was that big it would act more like a moat around a flippin' castle.

Whatever the end result looked like, the glamming-up, the styling and the coiffing were a big part of the fun of clubbing for me. While I enjoyed dancing and boy-watching, the very best part of going out was the dressing up. I adored piecing together an outfit that would turn heads.

Being the size I was at that time – an eighteen to twenty – that wasn't easy. After all, there wasn't much on offer in the shopping precinct for someone like me. The clothes that fitted would be dowdy and formless: definitely not the kind of fashion a girl in her teens would want to wear – and certainly not the kind of outfits a guy would want to see a girl in.

On a weekend, I'd trawl round the shops hunting for sexy outfits that would catch boys' eyes, but there was simply nothing in my size that I liked. All the larger lady shops in those days – well, there was only Evans – seemed to stock clothes that would make Kate Moss look fat. I don't know how they used to do it, but the cut was completely shapeless. Long on the parts you wanted to show, and short on the bits you wanted to cover. I still maintain that the fashion industry needs to come up with a fabulous range for curvy gals.

To make up for what I couldn't find, Mum would get outfits tailor-made for me. They were a sight to see. Everything that was designed for me was flamboyant, to say the least. I had a zebra-print combo, and a bright yellow canary outfit in PVC. Sure, I was big, but I wasn't going to let it stop me from having a good time.

My best college girlies Carla and Charlotte and I just loved getting our glad rags on and painting the town red. When the Blackpool illuminations went on, the nights got even better: with all those lights came the tourists. No offence to the Blackpool chappies, but out of season there were just the same ole faces, in the same ole places. Besides, you know what girls are like when they spy fresh men on the scene.

Our favourite hangout was Main Street. It was this massive venue that had loads of bars downstairs, while upstairs was The Business, which was a trendier bar that had a DJ spinning his tunes in a hollowed-out helicopter and cages all around the room with clubbers dancing in them. Needless to say, I never cage-danced, just in case people saw me and put me in Blackpool Zoo.

Main Street was always rammed to the rafters with boys doused in Jean Paul Gaultier aftershave, and dolled-up girls caked in spray-on body glitter that you seemed to find on your skin days afterwards, even after you'd had two showers, a bath and a body scrub.

Now the rule was, if you couldn't pull in Main Street, you had to drag yourself upstairs to The Business in a last-ditch attempt for a 2 a.m. snog. That was back when clubs used to play a slow number to round off the evening. Remember when they used to play that one last down-tempo song? Now all you get is banging music right till the end of the night. I say bring back the smoochy, the days of Boyz II Men blasting out 'End of the Road'.

In time, boys on the clubbing scene started to show me some attention. Yes, you did read that right, don't change your glasses: boys appeared to be interested. And one night, in The Business, I had my first proper kiss. Yep, sound the fanfare, folks: Jodie Prenger finally gets a snog!

The lucky guy to get some Jodie time was a fella called Greg. Even now, I get giggly just thinking about it. Finally, after watching Jason and Kylie kissing on *Neighbours*, telling myself, 'That's how you do it,' it was my turn. I may not have looked like Kylie and he wasn't anything like Jason Donovan, but it was my first kiss.

Although this was definitely a monumental occasion in my life, the details are a bit hazy, no doubt due to the ridiculous amount of alcohol I had consumed during the evening – for me. Ooh, I'd had at least four. All I can remember is that he was blond and handsome (or am I just imagining Jason Donovan?). I liked blonds and I thought he was very cute. I can't recall how we got talking, but I do remember it was almost two in the morning, which meant it was that time of the night when everyone was trying to latch on to anything they could get before kicking-out time.

Anyway, as the slow-dance music started – that smoochy Boyz II Men number coming on – we must have somehow hooked up and started kissing. Yes, kissing. Can you believe it? I flaming well couldn't. A real-life boy was puckering up and giving my lips a good seeing-to. This was unbelievable.

It was what I had been waiting for, for sixteen years of my life. A good old-fashioned snog. Obviously, I wasn't really sure what I was doing, but I just bluffed my way through it. I'd seen my fair share of romcoms over the years, so I had picked up a few tips about kissing technique. Whether I used any of them there and then, I can't tell you. I can't even remember if I closed my eyes during the kiss or whether I left them open to make sure that I wasn't dreaming.

Whatever I did, I loved every minute. In fact, just to make sure the moment lasted a lot longer and that Greg didn't have a chance to get away, I wrapped my arms around him and made sure there was no escape.

That most tender embrace ended suddenly when the lights came up: that horrible moment of the night when the stark bright light brings you back to earth with a bump. In that split second, all the magic disappeared. We jolted back from each other, both a little embarrassed.

It's funny, isn't it? When you're snogging in a club and the coloured lights are flashing all around, you feel like you're in this magical place, and everything and everyone seems out of this world. And then when the music stops and the room is lit up, you realize that you're not actually in heaven at all, but in a dirty, grubby club with glasses and bottles scattered around you on the floor.

Amazingly, Greg was just as cute in the bright lights, which was a bonus. What he thought of me, I don't know. I never will, because I never saw him again after that – I wouldn't be surprised if he'd moved out of Blackpool. But I didn't mind. Greg was my first kiss. And that's what I cared about.

Finally, I felt like my life had turned a corner. Yes, I was still larger than life, but I had been able to pull a guy. That was a major achievement. It was like climbing Mount Everest and almost reaching the top.

For days afterwards, I would think about that kiss and imagine it was the best one I would ever have. As it turned out, of course, it wasn't. At that time, though, even a peck on the cheek would have had me come over all peculiar.

Thanks to Greg, the curse had been broken. Now, there was no going back.

14

A Taste of Love

My seventeenth birthday saw me sign up for driving lessons. My parents, very generously, bought me a hot pink jeep, and I couldn't wait to pass my test to get my hands on it.

It was all wrapped up with ribbons on the morning I excitedly left the house to demonstrate my motoring skills to the examiner. Less than an hour later, I was back. The ribbons mocked me as I rushed past the jeep into the kitchen, where I sobbed to my mum that I'd failed the test for driving too slowly.

Happily, back then you could reschedule it really quickly, and by the evening I was the proud owner of the jeep, having passed my test that same afternoon.

The car was the campest thing you've ever seen. Not only was it neon pink, but it also had a personalized number plate that my nan had bought me, which read: 'J1odyp'. It looked just like a Barbie car, but as we all know, I ain't no Barbie.

As if to prove the point, as well as studying for the BTEC at Fylde, I was also gaining another qualification at the same time – as a nail technician. I always thought it would be 'good to fall back on'. Even at college, where we were being trained for careers in the entertainment industry, we were told what a fickle business it was we were going into.

I enjoyed doing people's nails. I say 'nails' – some of them were more like talons. To this day, I still do my own and my friends' nails. It's proved a surprisingly useful skill.

Once I got my mitts on my car, my mates and I used to skive off the really boring lessons at college and cruise around in the jeep. It took me a while to get the hang of the driving lark – in fact, my mum used to say to me, 'That car's had more facelifts than Joan Rivers,' and she wasn't far wrong. Fortunately, they were never serious scrapes.

My first summer at college was the best summer ever. That year, the sun was shining, the birds were tweeting ... and I fell deeply in love. His name was Bobby; we met in Main Street one hot night. Funnily enough, it turned out that he went to school with my good friend Alison (a great lass: we've always been the best of mates). Bobby and I really hit it off together.

All through that summer, we used to go riding around in my jeep and have a right laugh. It was a really special time for me and I look back on it fondly. As we tore through the streets of Blackpool and the quieter lanes outside of town, I remember thinking to myself that maybe I had found Mr Right at last.

There was one day that I will never forget during those months. I will always remember it as one of my happiest. Bobby and I were cruising around town as usual, but this time we were armed with these two massive water pistols. Whenever we saw someone, we started shooting at them as we drove by. I feel bad when I think about it now – but I did use mineral water, does that make it any better?

Of course, we thought we were the funniest people in the world. Our victims probably thought we were a right couple of knob jockeys. We didn't have a care as we caused havoc; we were like a junior version of Bonnie and Clyde. We were young and in love and barely mindful of anything else.

However, we were brought back to earth with a massive bump when we got home that evening – to find a police car waiting for us. Apparently, some woman I had shot in the bum had reported us. What a killjoy, eh?

She told the police that a pink jeep had whizzed past her and the next thing she knew, she was soaking wet. Even though she said she wasn't able to identify the culprits, the police didn't have a hard time working out who was involved – as I was the only person in Blackpool to own a garish pink jeep with a spray-painted pink rhino on the back wheel cover with big lettering saying 'Pink Lady'.

Bobby came away with us Prengers on holiday that summer, and all was going well. It was a serious relationship and we spoke about our future and confessed that we both looked forward to being together for ever.

As often seems to happen, though, just as I thought life was going brilliantly, everything changed – and not for the better. When we got home, Bobby's mum told him that his dad had been killed in a car accident. From that moment on, things were never the same.

The loss of his father hit him badly. It's one of the worst things that can ever happen to anyone, and the last person in the world I wanted it to happen to was the guy I loved. Bobby became introverted and wouldn't talk to me about things. At first, I just took it as his way of dealing with the situation – after all, people deal with grief in so many different ways. But then I started to realize that something was wrong between us. We'd drifted apart.

Not long afterwards, a mate told me that she had heard that Bobby had got off with another girl. I didn't know whether to believe it or not. Regardless, when you're a teenager, and it's your first love, you might as well have told me that the world was going to end in 0.2 seconds. I wanted to confront him about it but, despite myself, I avoided talking about it. I still loved him. I didn't want to break up. I was willing to patch our relationship together so we could be happy again.

Yet it wasn't that simple. It turned out Bobby wanted to

end it. He told me it was over, that he wanted to have nothing more to do with me.

Heartbroken, I tore round to his house and begged him to take me back.

'I love you, I love you,' I pleaded, as I tried to squeeze through his door. But he wouldn't listen and literally shut the door in my face, leaving me crying my eyes out in his front garden.

A day or two later, I tried to convince him to take me back. This time, there was a glimmer of hope and he said we could try again. And so we started to date, but it was never the same as before. One night, when I was out with the girls, I saw him in a bar – with his hand on another girl's bum. I realized then that it was over, even if my heart wasn't ready for it to be. I knew that I couldn't let him treat me like rubbish.

After my emotions had been battered once again, I turned to the one thing that always put a smile on my face: my old Irish mate Choc O'Late. A nice brew and a bar of Wispa could make the worst pain fade away. A mouthful of the sweet stuff was sometimes the greatest feeling in the world, while boys had proved time and again that they could be a whole lot of trouble. Now, if only men were made of chocolate. Wouldn't the world be a better place?

After we broke up, I went back to the clubbing scene, keener than ever to find a good man. I think my need for a boyfriend was rooted in my insecurities. As many girls do, I believed that if someone – anyone – loved me, then maybe I could start to love myself. I was relying on men to make me feel accepted.

Ironically, most of my dealings with fellas, throughout the course of my life, have left me more hurt and damaged than if I'd never got involved with them in the first place. Typical, isn't it?

After my relationship with Bobby, I had hoped that I would

now have legions of blokes falling over themselves to get to know me. But that wasn't the way it worked out. The thing was, although I looked confident and outgoing, I was still at heart a shy girl who couldn't make the first move.

That episode with the fairground guy had affected me more deeply than I had realized at the time. Now, when I saw men I liked, I immediately disregarded them, thinking that there was no damn way in the world they'd ever be interested in me. I was insecure and thought that no right-minded boy would want to go out with a big fat thing like me.

At this point in time, I hadn't come out of myself. I hadn't yet learned the gift of the gab. Aside from the odd snog, which would momentarily raise my spirits, no blokes really came anywhere near me.

Naturally, not all of those encounters were worth writing home about. I remember kissing this one guy while the song 'No Limits' by 2 Unlimited played in the background. It was the most bizarre experience I have ever had, because this lad insisted on kissing me in time to the music. Imagine how off-putting it is to have a chap sticking his tongue into your mouth in rhythm to 'No, no; no, no, no, no ...'

Then things suddenly started to look up.

One night, my mates and I hit the town and headed to the Palace. Now, you should know that the Palace is considered by Blackpool natives as a right old meat market. It was popular with the tourists, and the guys there were clearly looking for a no-strings holiday romance. It was tacky, but my mates and I didn't mind. With a drink in us, we could have had a good time in a phone box. That's just the way we were.

While we were boogying on the dance floor, I caught sight of a guy I thought was absolutely stunning. He was really, *really* good-looking: tall and dark, and a little on the beefy side.

Later, I discovered that he was as nice in personality as he was in appearance. He was older than me, around twenty-three or twenty-four. Funnily enough, I could tell that even before he told me, because he seemed a lot more sorted than most of the guys I'd met before. Mark said that he was a builder, who had done a bit of modelling work in his time, and that he had his own house, all of which got big ticks on my list of man criteria. Finally, I'd stumbled across a guy who seemed to know what he wanted from life and wasn't some boozed-up tearaway who wanted to go out on the lash all the time.

Although we could barely hear in the club, we spent most of the night chatting; not snogging, just talking about this and that. When the evening came to an end, I was hoping that something might happen between us. This guy seemed to be absolutely perfect, and we had connected. He was funny and he was sexy and he appeared to have a stable life. More importantly, he seemed interested in me. Surely there had to be something wrong with him?

When the lights came up, he told me that he wanted to take my number, which I gave him without hesitation. I was quaking in my shoes. This was almost like a relationship ... okay, so I was jumping the gun a little bit. Naturally, I played it cool in front of him. We demurely kissed each other goodbye – and then I joined my mates again and jumped up and down on the spot, unable to fathom what had happened.

Being Jodie, as soon as I'd headed home, doubts began to creep into my mind. Just because he took my number didn't necessarily mean that he was going to call. And the number he gave me could easily not have been his. Maybe it was all a big joke.

When I was back in my bedroom, I thought about dialling his number, just to see if he was pulling my leg or not. Luckily, I managed to talk myself out of it. If it was a fake number, then my heart would be broken. But if it was the right number, he'd think I was some crazy man-hungry loon who was totally uncool. After all, there's a rule about making that first phone call, as in 'don't call the same night or you'll end up looking like a stalker'.

By the way, what is it with all the rules about phone calls and texts when you're dating, or maybe I should say trying to date? I still don't get it. You take a fella's number, but then what do you do with it? 'They' say wait a day to contact him; they say if he texts you back, then you have to wait at least an hour to respond, and then you should text back only a short message. I say if two people want to talk, let 'em: stuff these rules.

Having said that, one sticks: the don't-call-or-text-if-you're-drunk rule. Oh come on, we have all done it ... and then woken up in the morning, looked at our phones and wished that at the very point we'd dialled the number, the ground had opened up and swallowed us.

The night I met Mark, I lay awake in bed, unable to sleep, recapping what had happened during the evening. If he was genuinely into me, then things were really coming together.

I must have been smiling like a maniac as I lay there, thinking about all the dates we could go on – and all the romance I had to look forward to. No one had ever bought me flowers, so I was definitely hoping for that; although to be honest, as far as I was concerned, Mark could sidestep the floral tributes and go straight for the Milk Tray. The box with two layers, so I could eat the bottom layer and leave the top layer full, so it would look like I had hardly been at 'em. That's a way to Jodie's heart.

The next day, I was still on cloud nine. Then the telephone rang and my cloud status went into double digits. What we spoke about, I couldn't possibly tell you, but by the end of the call, we had agreed to meet again. That was it. From that moment on, we were an item.

Mark was a lovely chap – one of those bona fide nice guys.

My parents loved him too. He was so much more mature than most of the lads you saw in Blackpool, and a lot more settled. For a time, I found that very attractive. We went to restaurants, savoured delicious meals and he treated me like a lady. More importantly, he told me I was beautiful and that he loved me, all of me. Not bad going for a girl who was twice the size of him.

But as much as I enjoyed going out with him, something wasn't quite right. It had nothing to do with him; it was me – as clichéd as that sounds. He was so into me, so loving, and there were times when he even said to me, 'Jodie, I could marry you tomorrow.' Unfortunately, all I could think about when he said that was that song by Garth Brooks, 'Tomorrow Never Comes'.

It wasn't that I didn't love him. In many ways, I did. He made me feel special and wonderful, more so than I had ever felt before. He helped me to wipe away all the pain, all the unhappiness that had been caused by a lifetime's worth of disappointments. What can I say? He made me feel like a natural woman.

Nevertheless, I was so young – not even twenty yet. He was twenty-four and had already achieved lots of what he wanted to do in life. He had his job, his money and his house. All he wanted now was to find that special someone with whom he could share it.

He thought he'd found that person in me. I was so chuffed that he considered me worthy of being The One, but for me, my life hadn't got going yet. There were things I needed to do, places I wanted to see. Even more men I might date. I had to explore every avenue before I shut all other doors. To settle down and get married at that point was the wrong thing to do. I knew it.

In the past, I'd always thought that if some man was stupid enough to fall in love with me, then I'd snap him up straight away. But for the first time in my life, I heard that voice in my head. Don't worry, I haven't gone crazy: I mean that little voice inside all of us that you have to listen to every now and again. It was telling me that now wasn't the time for all this.

Meeting Mark gave me a brand-new confidence – a confidence I don't think anyone else could have given me back then. It fuelled my dreams. I knew that it wouldn't be fair to give Mark the impression that I was ready to settle down. For after much thought, I realized that there was no way I could.

Ten months after getting together, Mark and I went our separate ways. We did so on good terms. In fact, he got in touch with me around four years ago, and we started seeing each other again for a time. But it just wasn't the same. It wasn't as passionate. He was exactly the same lovely man I had met all those years ago. I was a different person.

I am a believer in the theory that people grow, people change, and that with every passing moment you develop into the person you will one day become.

Over the years, I have gone from being a shy kid to someone who has found some belief in themselves. It hasn't been an easy journey. Yet as you get older, you learn how to deal with the knocks you suffer along the way. Whether you've been beaten down by boys, or by being overweight, or by not getting certain auditions, or by any other thing, all those setbacks help you to develop skin thicker than an elephant's elbow.

Little did I know it then, but I was going to need all my inner strength for the challenges that lay ahead.

15

Let Me Entertain You

had always dreamed of becoming some kind of entertainer. Dancing was the thing I'd loved when I was a child, but soon – with my experiences in the school choir and my roles in musicals – singing overtook it as a passion. By the time my years at Fylde College drew to a close, I knew for a fact that singing was my bag.

Of course, music had always been a big part of my life. I'd grown up loving Michael Jackson – some might say to excess. And while I might have been rubbish at multiplication, I was fab at picking up melodies. I can play the piano by ear – well, not in a literal sense as that would hurt, but if I hear a tune, I can pick it out on a keyboard. Nevertheless, I would still love to learn how to read music properly.

My mum did try to encourage me to do so when I was younger, kindly arranging one-to-one tutorials with a piano teacher for me, but it was a disaster. At that point, I wasn't fussed about doing it in the slightest. Every time the piano teacher came round, I would fake a headache and lie on the couch. While I was pretending to be asleep, the poor guy would just continue playing.

My mum would say to him, 'Don't worry about hanging around,' but he wouldn't hear of it and would murmur in response, 'I'll stay in case she wakes up.'

I never did. Once the hour was up, the chap would whisper

to my mum, 'Maybe she'll be feeling better next time.' Of course, I never was.

Although my nan liked to get up and do a turn for the guests at the hotel, the rest of my family were not particularly that way inclined. That said, my Aunty Margaret married a guy called Jim, whose dad wrote the theme tune to 'Always Coca-Cola'. So somewhere in my family tree there were traces of musicality, however distant.

Music and performing certainly felt like they were in my blood. I was still quite shy at this time when it came to dealing with people on an ordinary basis, so my adventures on stage made me realize that I had a bit of a Jekyll-and-Hyde character. I could barely say boo to some people in 'real' life, but when I hit the stage, I came alive. There I sang with confidence and felt so at home.

After graduating from Fylde, I decided to enter a local talent contest. It was a bit like *Britain's Got Talent*, but on a much smaller scale – and worse. I came second. The host, a well-known comedian called Jack Diamond, who used to be engaged to Julie Goodyear, found it hard to pronounce my surname, so he'd introduce me on stage as 'a Dutch ruptured clog dancer', because of my Dutch heritage.

After that, I decided to give myself a stage name to make it easier on everyone. I opted for Jodie Moore. No, not because I thought I looked like Demi. It was all part of a hilarious stage gag, where I'd say to the audience, 'Do you want some more?' ... and that's what I'd give 'em.

As it turned out, in spite of his trouble with my name, Jack Diamond took a real shine to me. He gave me a lot of support: introducing me to agents; giving me loads of great advice about 'the business'; and telling me that I should take up singing professionally. It was food for thought.

Living in Blackpool, what better place was there to cut my teeth than in the local working men's clubs and gay bars? You couldn't have asked for a more varied crowd.

Consequently, I decided to take the plunge and establish my own cabaret act.

Dad helped me out with the two grand I needed to buy the required equipment, and he even volunteered to chauffeur me to all the venues. Let me say now, thank you, Dad, for all the help you've ever given me. I couldn't have done it without you.

My first show was at Dollies bar in Blackpool, a smoky saloon bar that was definitely a one-stop wonder: I never went back.

In the two weeks leading up to the gig, I was nervous as hell. I bought all my backing-track CDs and worked hard on choosing the songs I was going to sing on the night. I decided that tracks from the musicals were the way forward. After all, doesn't everyone like songs from the shows? I was about to find out.

When I arrived at the bar, I was quaking in my sparkly shoes, attired in a brand new spangly outfit. This was my first time out on stage on my own and I was terrified. Glancing at the crowd, I grew even more nervous. They seemed like a tough bunch, the kind who had been drinking there for thirty years or so and probably wouldn't take kindly to some whippersnapper in an eyesore of a dress banging out a few tunes. They would take, I anticipated, some warming up.

When it became time for me to take to the stage, I was all fingers and thumbs as I fiddled nervously with the microphone stand.

'Hey up,' I said. 'How's you all doing?'

There was no response. Not a good start. Without any further ado, I launched into my set, kicking off with 'Don't Cry For Me Argentina' from *Evita*. I bombed. The crowd might as well have been cardboard cut-outs. No one seemed at all interested in what I was doing on stage, and instead they continued to have conversations amongst themselves, puffing away on their fags and supping their ale.

On stage, it felt like the longest forty-five minutes ever. Halfway through one song, I wished that I was wearing Dorothy's red slippers, so that I could tap my heels together and transport myself home.

Eventually, I reached the end of my set and I said my goodbyes. The trickle of applause that I received said it all. But hey, it was my first time. As far as I was concerned, I had done a good job. I had sung the songs brilliantly, I had put on a bit of a show – it wasn't my fault that the clientele were as dull as ditchwater. In fact, I was quite chuffed with myself.

As Dad drove me home, I replayed the evening in my head and I realized that I had actually enjoyed myself. Yes, I'd been petrified by the whole experience, but I had loved being under the spotlights, and best of all I'd really relished belting out those old show tunes. Perhaps even more incredible was the fact that I'd been paid for doing what I loved.

Sadly, it took a while for my shows to take off. At one gig, in Manchester, when we pulled up outside the venue, Mum and Dad told me they didn't want me to go in. The place looked like a mental asylum and had metal bars on all the windows. In fairness, you could understand why as the area it was in wasn't exactly the nicest. It was the kind of neighbourhood where you had to park your car near the door, so that you could keep an eye on it in case the local kids tried to nick your wheels. Mum and Dad begged me not to do the show, but I'd agreed to perform – and that's what I was going to do.

Inside, the bar was no better. The stage had one of those metal grilles across the front, in case the crowd got rowdy and felt like throwing an ashtray at you. Consequently, the stage resembled an upright coffin. To give you an even clearer picture of the place, it was the kind of club where, during the show, they would sell raffle tickets to the punters; the grand prize was a slab of meat. Yum. Nevertheless, I still went on and did the gig. Ever the professional, eh?

Another time in Manchester, I came face to face with a right rowdy bunch of buggers. They were harmless, but I swear it felt like I was playing a hecklers' convention or something, as they all had something to say during the show.

I started off with a rather jovial: 'Does anyone like songs from the musicals?'

The reply? A monotone 'No!', which obviously set me off on a bad footing.

Undeterred, I carried on anyway, launching into 'Don't Cry For Me Argentina'. Needless to say, they hated me. Little did I know then that one day I would be singing a song from *Evita* for the composer himself, Andrew Lloyd Webber. That outcome was a million miles away from that particular gig.

In the early days, I would sing around twenty-five songs, which must have been a nightmare for those crowds who hated show tunes. My favourites were the Stevie Wonder tracks, but I also performed Vera Lynn, Bette Midler, Liza Minnelli … all the classics. As time went on and I gained more confidence on stage, I whittled the number down to around nine – and I started to fill in between songs with a bit of banter.

This was how I learned the gift of the gab – even though, at times, I was still trying to hide behind the microphone stand. Let me tell you, at 18 stone, that isn't bloody easy.

Everywhere I went, there'd always be some clever dick who thought he could be funny and make some sarky comment about my size. I remember in one club, I got up on stage and this cheeky fella called out, 'Bloody hell, love, that stage moved when you came on.' Then another shouted, 'Fookin' hell, I thought it was going to cave in!'

I'm not going to lie: the comments hurt me a lot. When I was on stage, I'd laugh it off, but once I was home and alone in my bed, I used to sob myself to sleep.

Then again, what did I expect? I was a fat bird and I guess, in some ways, I was asking for it, especially entering the world of working men's clubs. They were notoriously tough gigs. I knew I just had to push through and not let them destroy me.

As a result, over time, I developed a bit of a comedy routine to use as a defence mechanism ... and it worked. When someone made an unkind comment, I'd hit back with a gag like: 'My bum used to look big in this. Now it looks big in everything.' Amazingly, the crowds grew to like me, even if they still couldn't give a toss about what I was singing.

Around this time, I started to hang out with a bunch of lads I knew from college, who were in a band called Waterfront. It was with them that I had an experience that almost cost us our lives, and definitely lost us our eyebrows.

The lead singer of Waterfront was a guy called Mark, whom I dated for a while. Like in the Kylie and Robbie song 'Kids', though, it was the drummer who truly stole my heart. Ryan was cute, and a real Jack the Lad with a cheeky glint in his eye: the perfect combination for any girl.

Sadly, what with me being a ten-ton Tessie, he didn't appear to be interested. Well, not in the way I wanted him to be, anyway. We were the best of mates, however, and, as I'd found with Gavin, that was at least something. But more about him later.

In the meantime, back to Mark. One winter evening, during our relationship, Mark and I were round at his mum's house, together with his mate Steve, clearing out his mum's garden. In between swigs of Tetley tea, we chucked rubbish and loose tree branches and twigs on to a big bonfire. Once the garden had been cleared of all the debris, we started removing stuff like old papers and cardboard boxes from the garage and throwing them on the crackling fire.

Our tasks completed, we sat down on our camper seats and savoured the rest of our warm drinks, enjoying the heat of the fire on our faces.

All of a sudden, there was a sound that I still remember to this day: you could hear the air being sucked in, then a massive bang, and then a whoosh of what I can only describe as pure white heat around us. The next thing I knew, I was rolling around on the grass, clutching my face and feeling very, very hot. I could hear Steve and Mark groaning to my side and yelling that their faces were on fire.

'What's going on?' I thought. 'Has there been an explosion?'

Amid the confusion, one of the boys sensibly suggested that we should run next door to the hospital and get ourselves checked out. How lucky is that: Mark's mum lived right next door to A & E, the very place we needed to head to – and fast. As it turned out, it was a bloody good thing we got there as quickly as we did because the doctors were extremely concerned about our injuries when they saw us.

Of course, that made me even more anxious because I still wasn't sure what had happened to my face or what I looked like. I'd gathered by now that we had been involved in some kind of fire-related incident, but it wasn't clear why it had occurred. It later transpired that the cardboard boxes we had thrown on the fire had actually contained aerosol cans, which had exploded in the heat.

I had a million and one things running through my head. Once I had computed that fire was involved, I immediately assumed that I had been left hideously disfigured, and that I'd have to live my life like Freddy Krueger, or wear a mask like the Phantom of the Opera. I hadn't seen my face in a reflective surface at this point, but I could smell singed hair and I noticed that the front of my fleece had totally melted. If that's what my fleece looked like, what state was my face in? Had it melted off? Was I scarred forever more?

I kept saying to the boys, 'My face, my face – is my face okay?' but they were too preoccupied with their own agony to respond.

The more I worried about my face and the prospect of being horrifically disfigured, the more panicked I became.

I screamed out for my mum. She was the only one who would be able to calm me down. The medics tried, telling me that my parents were already on their way.

While I waited for them, the doctors took me into a room where there was a special sink for me to dip my face. It had two taps that would wash water over my flaming skin. I don't have a physical memory of it being painful, but I do recall that I simply couldn't bear to do it. The doctors kept insisting that I had to rinse the skin, and I kept rearing back like a horse that's scared out of its wits.

When I came up for breath one time, my mum and dad had arrived. They stopped short when they clapped eyes on me for the first time. Apparently, the skin was literally hanging off my face. The look on their faces scared me even more and tears started rolling down my burned cheeks – causing me even more agony. Mum later told me I looked horribly burned.

The doctors thought it would be best if the three of us were checked out at Preston's special burns unit. A hasty twenty-minute ride in an ambulance ensued. During the journey, Mark – who, very sweetly, always carried a picture of me in his wallet – pulled out my photograph. It was the last thing I wanted to see. As I gazed at my clear smiling face, I wondered if I was ever going to look like that again. I already had to deal with the fact I was overweight; could I handle having to cover up my face too?

In the end, our injuries weren't as bad as the doctors had first feared. I had no permanent scars, but I was left temporarily with just two stubs for eyebrows, no eyelashes or nostril hair, and I had lost some hair from the front of my head. I looked like I had alopecia.

Amid all this madness, Mark's mum suddenly appeared, carrying a tin-foil package, and asked us earnestly, 'Does anyone want any garlic bread?'

If I hadn't been in so much pain, I would have laughed.

And if I hadn't been in so much agony, I would have said, 'Yes, give it here.'

In the weeks after the accident, life was tough. I had to have a skin graft, and regularly coat my face in paraffin oil. We were advised not to go out, which was a nightmare for us as we were all partygoers, but it was sensible advice as black soot continued to seep out of our pores all that time.

It took a long while for the injuries to heal. I remember thinking, 'If the burns don't clear up, is that my career in showbiz out the window?' It really didn't bear thinking about.

Luckily, within two months, all was back to normal. Sadly, my relationship with Mark wasn't, and we split shortly afterwards. It was on good terms, though, and we still catch up every now and then.

16

Working Girl

Once I was back at work, my gigs improved massively. I think this was mostly because I hit the gay scene. With my over-the-top hairpieces, eyelashes and outfits, it was like the mothership coming home.

One of my favourite venues was the Mardi Gras in Blackpool, a really gorgeous old-fashioned gay bar frequented by the loveliest people you could ever meet. I don't know what it was about them, but they just 'got' me there. I'm not sure if it was the songs they liked, or the way I carried myself, or because I looked like a big old drag queen ... they just seemed to adore my shows. Then again, I've always been very camp.

I made some great friends there, such as a drag queen called Stella Artois, who is hilarious and does a turn at the club every week. She did a version of 'As Long As He Needs Me' when I was on *I'd Do Anything*, but something tells me the word 'long' meant something very different in her interpretation.

The Mardi Gras is a wonderful bar, mainly because it has kept its traditional charm while the world around it has moved on. While other clubs have had their interiors modernized and stripped of all personality, the Mardi Gras hasn't changed all that much over the decades. The stage still has the same red curtain that has hung there for the past twenty years or so. It's a small and intimate venue, and it has its own crew of regulars, which is worth something in this day and age. They've always been great audiences at the Mardi Gras, so I have had many memorable nights there.

In playing bars like the Mardi Gras and another called Funny Girls, I learned a lot about myself. It's a weird thing to say, but performing in these venues was like me coming out. No, Mum, before you start shopping for a toolbox and dungarees, I'm not a lesbian. For the first time, I simply felt totally at ease with myself. I didn't think anyone was judging me. I was big – and the crowds seemed to embrace that. The gay scene was definitely the place where I truly came alive, where I could just be me, singing my camp tunes, wearing my flamboyant frocks, and being cheeky with the boys, without fear of looking like a silly sod and being told as much.

Performing on the gay-bar circuit also had its perks. When you did a turn, it was usually before or after the stripper came on, which meant you had to share the dressing room with them. (Of course, when I say 'dressing room', I mean whatever space out the back there was for us to get ready in.)

Naturally, being a lady, I kept my eyes to myself. Yeah, right. I couldn't keep my eyes off those buff studs as they were getting changed. Having seen the preparation these guys put themselves through first-hand, I have to say it was pretty intense. Some would take Viagra in order to get themselves, er, up. And then to keep their ding dong standing to attention, they'd tie a pair of tights around it.

I remember one time I was doing a gig with three strippers, and I just didn't know where to look. They were all standing there totally naked, preparing themselves for their show. I kept focusing on the clock, while applying my make-up haphazardly. By show time, I had plastered my face with so much slap I looked like Dame Edna Everage on heat.

Sadly, none of the strippers I met ever asked me for a date – but then they were either gay or drop-dead gorgeous or both, so I was never really expecting a request.

It was around this time that I had a theatrical experience that I will treasure all my life. I took the role of Lottie Ames in the Premier Theatre Company's production of *Mack and Mabel*, which was staged at the Blackpool Grand in June 2000. I love that musical. Premier was an amateur group, but they invested lots of money in the show and it was of a really high standard, so I had no regrets whatsoever about signing up.

Almost the best bit, in fact, was being part of a cast again. It's a lonely thing to be a cabaret singer. No matter how much banter you share with the audience, you're out there on your own, and you pack up and go home on your own too. It was quite something to feel part of a theatre family again, and it reminded me just how much I adored performing in musicals. It was something I wasn't to forget.

In the meantime, though, now that I'd got a name for myself on the circuit, the cabaret work came flooding in. Over the course of two or three years, I did loads of shows, way too many to mention here. However, like any job, there were some gigs that definitely stick in my mind.

Such as the time I played Strangeways Prison. Before the right-wing press go up in arms, no, I wasn't entertaining the crims, it was actually for the wardens' staff party. I had to get changed in a cell. Talk about glamour, eh?

Then there was the time I performed at a transvestite convention. No, really, I did. The minute I stepped out on stage, I realized I was dying on my arse. I'm not sure why, but these guys – sorry, girls – just weren't warming to me. From what I could see, they were all trying to be refined and sophisticated and very ladylike, and I don't think my natural drag look went down well with them.

The thing was, if you looked past the make-up, you could see in their eyes that they wanted to whip off their wigs and let loose, but they just wouldn't. In a last-ditch attempt to get the girls up and dancing, I gave them a burst of Shania

Twain's 'Man, I Feel Like A Woman'. And you know what? That's all it took. Those ladies were up and dancing around their handbags for the rest of the night.

Another memorable gig was at a hotel in Blackpool, to which I took my mum along for moral support. Halfway through my first number, I noticed one of the guests in the audience get up from her seat, walk across the room, snog this random guy and then sit back down again.

'That's weird,' I thought, trying to keep my mind on the song.

Then the same woman got up again and went and kissed another guy. I'm not sure if it was obvious to everyone around me, but I became fixated on what was unfolding in front of me.

That's me all over: I'm at my happiest when I'm watching folks. I'd be quite content to spend my days sitting in a park wearing a pair of comfy slippers, munching my way through a bag of roasted nuts and watching the world go by.

Anyway, something rather fishy was clearly going on. More and more people started kissing each other. Observing my mum, I noticed she had become increasingly uncomfortable. Something very odd was happening. I couldn't wait to get offstage, to: one, find out what was going on; and two, if it was dodgy, get the hell out of there.

As it turned out, we discovered that the hotel was a place where people came to have a massive orgy. The minute my turn was finished, the guests were off and they jumped on each other. Luckily, my mum and I managed to escape in the nick of time.

On the whole, my cabaret gigs have always been pretty okay. With that sort of scene, you never expect four-star service or accommodation. Having said that, I have sometimes still been shocked by the conditions, and by the behaviour of some of the clientele. I've played at clubs where the entire place has stunk of pee, and in many places I've had to get changed in stinky toilets.

The worst gig I did was at a working men's club in north Wales – where the men were men and the sheep were scared. Halfway through my set, this guy waddled up to the front of the stage, smiling. At first, I was pleased, as it looked like he was enjoying the show – but I was wrong. He reached up, took my hand ... and started to suck my finger. I was disgusted and pulled my hand back as fast as I could. It was so painful having to continue with my set, as I was desperate to get offstage and give my hand a good wash.

My act became much more comedy-based over time. Don't get me wrong, I never told a single joke, but I loved having a right good laugh with the audience. Consequently, I was considered in the business as a brilliant warm-up act, and my agent at the time landed me several gigs on that basis.

They were great jobs, as I got to work with people like Ricky Tomlinson at the Liverpool Empire Theatre, where I also met his brother. You wouldn't believe how much they look alike, and I mean 'lookalike'; I couldn't tell them apart. There were many other stars that I worked with too: Ken Dodd, Frank Carson, Joe Pasquale, Billy Pierce and Bernard Manning, to name but a few.

I never actually met Bernard properly because by the time he came on, I was dashing off to do another show. I remember his crowd was strange. My humour was a bit tame for them; I think they were waiting to hear some jokes about mother-in-laws – or worse.

The old hands like Joe Pasquale and Frank Carson were great. Really decent men, who were always very friendly, and gave me an insight into the life I really wanted. Seeing how successful and how loved they were gave me the hunger to do well. Of course, I wanted to sing. Comedy wasn't really my thing. That had just been a by-product that had got me through some nasty scrapes. I knew there was still a long way to go in my chosen career.

Luckily for me, jobs kept landing in my lap. As more and

more people and venues came to hear of me, I found myself doing two or three shows a night. See, people might think I had it easy by winning *I'd Do Anything* and a plum part, but I really did graft in the years beforehand.

It was a wonderful learning experience. It was also a tough life. You have to rough it to get on, dragging your equipment from one venue to another, all by yourself. Fortunately, I had my dad to help me – without him, I don't know what I would have done.

In the autumn of 2000, spurred on by my enjoyment of *Mack and Mabel* and the thrill of being part of a big production, I scoured *The Stage* newspaper for adverts for musicals. I wanted to go back to my roots. It wasn't long before I spotted an open audition for *Spooktacular*, the Halloween ice extravaganza at Alton Towers, and took myself along to try out.

I was excited. Alton Towers is the closest thing we have to Disney World in Britain. Obviously, one thing was worrying me: the show was staged on ice. Now, being the size I was, it was hard enough to stay on two feet at the best of times. There sure as hell was no way I was going to be able to cope on ice skates. If I fell, I'd crack the bloody rink in two. I was gutted as that sank in, because the job would have been a good one.

But the angels must have been looking down on me. As the producers offered me a part, they said that my role would be a non-skating one. Result! Cinders could go to the ball after all. Apparently, I could wear golf shoes for the part of the evil witch.

So, I was off to freezing Derbyshire for the winter. As I wanted to be independent, I told my mum and dad that I would find and pay for my own place to live. With little money, I ended up in a caravan on a campsite near to the theme park.

Staying there was the single worst experience of my life. Worse even than that finger-sucker in north Wales. The caravan was cold and smelly and creepy, and it was full of earwigs and bugs. Whenever I tried to get to sleep, I became convinced that someone was trying to break in. If they had succeeded, they would have been in for a shock – there was nothing there to pinch, but there was a big fat girl shivering in the bed with cold and fear. Oh, I couldn't bear it. I hated living on my own, with just myself for company. I needed to be around people.

Fortunately, I'd made friends on the show with a guy called Toby Hinson. He was my knight in shining armour and took me away from all the misery. He told me I could come and stay with him at his hotel – just as friends, of course. Instantly, things were looking up.

I had a great time with Toby. Even though there wasn't much to do in the area, we could entertain ourselves. To be honest, most nights we'd just sit in eating Cajun chicken and diced potatoes. Simple tastes for simple folk.

Spooktacular ran for a month and was an amazing experience. It was my biggest job to date. The staging was high tech, with loads of fantastic props, special effects and costumes. We even had a Hollywood film star appear with us every night.

Now, don't get too excited. It wasn't Mel Gibson – but it was, in fact, the horse that appeared alongside him in the movie *Braveheart*. How cool is that? Even though he may have been a star of the silver screen, Todo, as he was called, wasn't shy about pooing all over the ice at least once a day. Mind you, me feeding him a bag of carrots every twenty-four hours probably didn't help, and he was also rather partial to a sweetie. Ah, you know what I'm like with animals. I can't help myself.

The families who came to see the show really loved it, booing the baddies and cheering on the goodies. There was such a buzz on set that it never felt like work. Going back home was definitely an anti-climax, even though it was lovely to be back in my own bed.

Yet as it turned out, I didn't have to wait long before another golden opportunity came my way. A short while after I'd moved back home, my mate Shelley – Gavin's sister – and I took a trip to London. Shelley was planning to audition for a job on one of those Disney cruise liners that travel down the coast of Florida, while I was just tagging along for the ride. I was looking forward to getting drunk in the big smoke. And that's exactly what we did.

Starting off our reckless night in All Bar One in Leicester Square, Shelley, our mate Sarah and I downed drink after drink, until we were as tipsy as giddy aunts and rather desperately flirting with men. We then stumbled through the bustling streets of London to a bar called Long Island Iced Tea, where we proceeded to slam-dunk as many drinks as they'd serve us, before ending our night of depravity by chowing down on a nice tasty kebab.

Unsurprisingly, the heady cocktail of drinks and manky food did not sit well in my tummy. Before you could say, 'Pass us a bucket,' I was chundering into my handbag. Classy, eh?

The next morning, I really paid for the night before. My head was thumping, my mouth was like the bottom of a birdcage and my stomach felt like the Roly Polys had been using it as a wrestling mat. I felt as sick as a dog. I was feeling ever so fragile, and the last thing I needed to see was a bright, shiny, happy face looking down at me, especially when it belonged to someone who was trying to get me out of bed.

Nonetheless, that's just the image I had as I lay in my pit. Somehow, Shelley had managed to wake up as fresh as a daisy after our big night. She was already washed and dressed for the audition as I attempted to open my eyes.

'So, are you coming?' she called out, far too perky for my liking.

'I don't think so,' I muttered in response, pulling the duvet over my head again.

Below: 'Can I fit this in my mouth in one go?' I wonder. Me with my nan.

Above: The platinum child: with my proud mum and dad at my christening.

Left: My first kiss, aged three.

Right: With my mum and brother Marko on the day he was born.

Above: With that outfit, how could I fail to win Pontin's disco-dancing competition? I'm on the right.

Above: Growing up, it was hard not to feel self-conscious about my size.

Right: Trying not to stick out like a sore thumb, aged twelve.

Left: Deirdre Barlow, eat your heart out: me, with Mum, dressed as 'mini Madeleine' – as usual.

Above: With my beloved nan and granddad on my eighteenth birthday.

Above: In costume for *Mack and Mabel:* the show was a turning point for me as a singer.

Left: Jodie Moore: cabaret star.

Left: With my fellow *Biggest Loser* contestants Ben *(centre)* and Lee *(right)*, and our trainer Angie *(front centre)*, in front of the *BL* mansion.

Above: The final weigh-in: my achievement was there for all to see.

Left: This really is a little black dress.

Above: The *I'd Do Anything* contestants: *(from left to right, back row)* Ashley, Jessie, Tara, host Graham Norton, Niamh, Keisha, Sam; *(front row)* Cleo, Rachel, Sarah, me, Amy, Fran.

Right: With Phill Jupitus after he led a comedy masterclass for us during the competition.

Left: Giving it my all in pursuit of my dream role – this is from the live final on 31 May 2008.

Above: On the programme after my win was announced.
I still can't thank you all enough.

Right: Backstage with
former Josephs Chris
Barton *(left)* and
Lewis Bradley.

Below: Fantastic, fantastic, fantastic: with friend
and *IDA* judge John Barrowman.

Above: Duetting with John at the Faenol Festival.

Left: My West End debut: on stage in the chorus of *Les Misérables*.

Below: At Andrew Lloyd Webber's birthday celebrations, with the Lord himself and 2007 *X Factor* runner-up Rhydian.

Above: Fixing my make-up in my dressing room at the Theatre Royal Drury Lane on *Oliver!*'s opening night.

Above: On stage with *(from left to right)* Burn Gorman, Ross McCormack, Rowan Atkinson and Harry Stott.

Above: Receiving – unbelievably – a standing ovation in the curtain call. The entire experience has been a dream come true.

'Come on, Jodie, you said you'd come along. I don't care how you feel.'

I tried to put up a fight, but I was weak and Shelley was very persuasive. However, I did warn her that it was her fault if I hurled chunks mid audition.

When we arrived at the Pineapple Dance Studios in central London, confusion reigned. Somehow, I was added to the audition list. This was a shock to me as I had had no intention whatsoever of trying out for the job: I was as far from looking like Snow White as you could get. In my sozzled state, however, I ended up thinking, 'What damage could it do to have a go anyway?' Even if I was suffering from the mother of all hangovers.

As fate would have it, luck was very much on my side. After I'd sung for the panel, I was asked to hang around for the next round, when I showed them my dancing skills. I was so surprised when they told me that they liked what they saw.

They kept asking me how I felt about heading out to the US and joining a Disney cruise. In all honesty, I hadn't really thought about it before that day, but on quick reflection, it seemed like a great opportunity. It was a prestigious job, working for one of the biggest entertainment companies in the world, and it was overseas. It seemed like the chance of a lifetime for a girl like me, who was desperate to kick-start a career in showbiz.

'Yes, I'd love it,' I told them in a breath (hoping they weren't close enough to smell it). 'I'm always up for a challenge!'

They thanked me for coming along, and told me I'd hear in due course as to whether or not I'd landed the job.

When we got back to Blackpool, back to the real world, I forgot all about the Disney experience. In my heart, I was convinced that I wouldn't be successful – I'd auditioned with a hangover, for goodness' sake. I hadn't been up to scratch, and I'd done no preparation whatsoever. At the end of the day, I told myself, it had been a good experience; I'd try harder next time.

But then, out of the blue, I got a call from the Disney company, telling me I had got the job, and that I was to star in their floating productions of *Disney Dreams*, *Hercules* and *Ghost Ship* as one of four principle performers.

At first, I thought it was a prank call. Could this be for real? Surely someone was just pulling my leg? The more I spoke to the person on the phone, however, the more I realized that this was genuine. After all, I didn't know anyone who could keep up such a good American accent for that amount of time.

I had won the role. I'd be moving to Canada in two months' time to start rehearsals. Not bad going for a girl who had been so hungover at the audition that she couldn't tell her left from her right on the dance floor!

Things were beginning to look up. And just around the corner, I had yet another surprise in store.

17

A Sinking Ship

U p until this point in my life, as you know, I hadn't had much luck in the men department. It seemed like my heart was always getting broken, or the guys I adored simply didn't give a monkey's about me in the first place.

In my bones, I felt like my luck was about to change. Surely I couldn't just lurch from one dysfunctional relationship to the next? When I met Darren on a night out, shortly after I'd landed the Disney job, I was hopeful that, finally, this was it.

Darren ticked all my boxes. He seemed a lovely, charming man, blessed with the gift of the gab. We started dating almost immediately – and hit it off so well that, not long afterwards, on my twenty-second birthday, he got down on one knee in my bedroom and proposed to me. Of course, being Jodie, and getting carried away with the moment, I said yes.

However, there was still the little matter of my imminent departure from the UK – I was still booked to spend a few months on the Disney cruises on the other side of the Atlantic Ocean. Now I faced a quandary. Should I relinquish the opportunity, so that I could be with my new fiancé? Or should I stick to my guns and take on America, or at the very least the east coast of it?

Mum thought I should give the job a go, as it was only a few months' work. Deep down, I knew she was right. After all, this could be the start of something, something I had waited for for so long. If Darren really loved me, he'd wait for me to return.

Head over heels in love, we threw an engagement party to celebrate our news, and so that I could say goodbye to everyone before I left for my rehearsals in Canada. I couldn't quite believe that all of a sudden my life, professionally and personally, was starting to work out.

My farewell to Darren was a tearful one. He told me he loved me and that he would miss me, but he also assured me that he knew this was my dream and that this was the path I had to take.

Of course, after all the excitement of the proposal and the party, upping and leaving now felt wrong. We'd only just got engaged, and here I was leaving my gorgeous fiancé behind. Was this the right thing to do? I was worried he might find someone else while I was away. Yet Darren reassured me that I would be the only person on his mind and that he'd be in constant touch while I was abroad.

And then it was time to go. It was my first trip to Canada, so I was really looking forward to seeing the country where my mum and dad had met, and where so many of my dad's family lived. As Nan had been when Mum left all those years before, Mum was sad to see me go, but she knew I'd come home. I was too much of a homebody to stay away for long.

On my first day of Disney rehearsals, I was full of fear, and nervous about what the future held for me. Luckily, the team I was part of turned out to be fantastic. I instantly became really good friends with Stephanie O'Brien, and with two lovely gay guys, Eric Shelley and Matthew O'Brien.

The four of us hit it off straight away, bouncing off one another like we'd known each other for years. In fact, we thought of ourselves as the four leads from the TV show *Will and Grace*: Steph was Grace, Eric was Jack, Matthew was Will, and I was crazy Karen.

The whole team got on brilliantly. We had a blast while we rehearsed the show, although there wasn't much to do in our spare time, aside from playing computer games – or tricks on each other. On one occasion, as a practical joke, I concealed a blood capsule about my person and then ran full pelt into a wall. Everyone thought I'd lost a tooth.

Since I'd left for Canada, Darren had been in touch regularly, just as he'd promised, which I thought was a good sign. He was missing me so much that he asked if he could come out to join me for a little bit. The rehearsal period in Canada lasted two whole months, so we had plenty of time before I set sail.

I told him I'd love him to visit. Naturally, I had described him to all my new friends and I wanted them to meet him. But that's when things started to go wrong.

When he arrived, he seemed like a totally different person to the Darren I'd known before. He was always asking where I was going and who I was doing stuff with. In honour of his arrival, I threw a Brits party for my American friends and served up silly nibbles like mini beans on toast, Cumberland sausages and vodka jellies. To start with, we were having a brilliant time. Only Darren didn't want to get involved. He seemed distant.

After a while, I joined him in the bedroom, where he was sitting on his own, and we ended up having a blazing row. Just like in a film, the music at the party in the next room stopped. Everyone froze.

Later, he apologized for his behaviour. I forgave him, but from then on, I was cautious.

After he went back to the UK, I carried on with my work, which I adored. Luckily, I didn't have much time to think about Darren. But when I did allow my thoughts to wander in his direction, I seriously started to reconsider my relationship with him. Although we were engaged to be married, I really didn't know that much about him.

In time, Darren came out to see me again. I was prepared to give it one more chance – he was my fiancé, after all – but things went from bad to worse. We argued constantly. The cracks were definitely straining the relationship, but even so, it seemed I wasn't quite ready to end it.

After Darren's brief and difficult visit, work became my priority as we set off on the cruise. The Disney cruises are a magical experience. The shows themselves were massive, big-budget spectacles, with wild pyrotechnics and huge show numbers, and the audiences loved every single minute.

Sometimes, we had celebrities like Whitney Houston and Jonathan Ross join us on the ship with their families. We even got to perform for one of America's former presidents, President Carter. His entourage booked out a whole floor on the boat, and when it came to the evening show, security was tighter than the seals on the ship itself.

The best audiences were of course the kids, who were in awe of what they saw. We had a lot of poorly children on the cruises, and that was humbling, because despite their problems, they came away smiling with joy, overwhelmed to be taking this once-in-a-lifetime trip. To see their faces so happy and carefree broke my heart, as I knew some of them might not pull through. It made me realize what was important in life.

I remember meeting this one little girl who was very sick. She didn't have long left to live. She told me that she was excited about being on the ship and couldn't believe that she was finally going to see all of her favourite characters on stage. I was determined that when she came to see the show, we would give 150 per cent, so that she would go away with some of the greatest memories she'd ever had.

Tragically, the little girl never made it to the show. It was absolutely heartbreaking. All I could think was that in spite of all the pain and discomfort she had been in when I'd met her, she had still managed to smile brighter than the sun. She was an inspirational person.

Mum, Dad, Marko and Darren came out to join me on the cruise. By this point, I had got things clear in my mind and I knew I didn't want to be with Darren any more. I felt I didn't know who this man was. I wanted him out of my life for ever. Thankfully, he soon was.

To tell you the truth, I was ashamed of what happened between us. I had always thought that I was reasonably clever, but in this instance I knew I had made a big mistake.

After we split up, I didn't hear from him for years. He got in touch after *The Biggest Loser*; I never replied. I don't wish him any harm – I wish him all the happiness in the world. I'm just very glad he is out of my life.

With Darren history, I threw myself into work so that I could put all the heartache to the back of my mind. What happened next, no one predicted, but it really put things into perspective for me.

Every so often, the Disney ships were put into dry dock for two weeks, while they were cleaned from top to bottom. It was during one of these spells that the news broke that two planes had smashed into the World Trade Center buildings in New York. Everyone was shocked, believing at first that it was just a terrible accident.

When it emerged that terrorists were behind the catastrophe, everyone went into panic mode. People were worried that Disney, that all-American flagship, could be the next target. I had been planning to head home in a few days for a short break, but flights across the country were grounded and cancelled.

The cruise liner was docked in Virginia, where some of the US Navy ships are based, so from where we were, we could see them all heading out into the ocean, in pursuit of vengeance. It was a terrifying experience. I was away from home and my loved ones, and it felt like we were in the middle of a war.

It was a very scary time. The fear of terrorism was such that one of our duties was to patrol for bombs, while parts of the ship were locked off, so that if a bomb did go off on board, that particular section wouldn't flood the rest of the ship. It was horrid.

A few days later, I was finally able to get a flight home. I just wanted to be with my family if all hell broke loose.

On the journey back to England, I thought about all those innocent people who had lost their lives in the disaster. They'd probably gone into work that morning and never even imagined that they'd never see another day. It made me realize how lucky I was to be alive. It also made me appreciate that life is short, and that I had to make the most of what I had: the love of my family, my health and my career. I was a lucky one.

A fortnight later, I was back out on the cruise ships. My aim for the next few months was to try to bring some happiness to the Americans. I felt better about myself. Darren was now just part of my past and I felt I could move on with my life.

After spending my very first Christmas away from home – lying on a beach, eating turkey burgers and playing volleyball – I decided I had had enough of my time on the ocean waves. When my Disney contract came to an end, I headed back to Blackpool, where I returned to the cabaret circuit, albeit in slightly classier venues.

After my experiences on the ships, though, I wasn't entirely happy. I'd done the cabaret scene to death over the past four or five years. I needed a new challenge. I wanted more from life. What I needed was another break ...

It came, literally, in the form of gigs at holiday resorts, with the Thomson travel company. It was a fabulous set-up. They'd fly me out to places like Rhodes and Cyprus for a few days, where I'd do the show, get a suntan and then head home again.

During my regular set for Thomson, I'd always sing the

Celine Dion song 'My Heart Will Go On', from the film *Titanic*. To help visualize the movie and its infamous scene on the ship's bow, I used to play Kate Winslet's Rose, and I'd pull a guy out of the crowd to play Leonardo Di Caprio's Jack, using the age-old line, 'Is that an iceberg in your pocket … ?' Then, for comedy effect, I'd pick the guy up and swing him around. It worked (almost) every time and the audiences loved it.

Indeed, some revellers enjoyed it so much that they got carried away with it themselves. One time, in Tenerife, I was in the middle of the skit and I chose this tiny Chinese man in the crowd as my Jack for the evening. He was so small that you could have rested a pint on his head. Just as I was about to pick him up, he outmanoeuvred me, grabbed hold of my middle and picked *me* off the floor and swung me around. I don't know where he found the strength, but bless that man for doing that.

Very occasionally, the gag fell flat with some of the punters. Like the time I did a show at the Edwardian Hotel in Blackpool. I'd reached the *Titanic* part of my routine and looked out into the crowd for a not-so-willing volunteer.

Spotting a likely lad, I stepped into the audience and bounded toward him. As I did so, his face became fearful. Before he had time to protest, I dragged him out of his seat, picked him up and swung him round. Instead of laughing his pants off, as usually happened, the poor unsuspecting fella let out a right old groan. The pressure of me swinging him around and holding him so tightly had split open the stitches he'd recently had administered to his shoulder. Oops.

A little while later, at a different gig, I grabbed another guy out of his chair – only to discover, too late, that he had a massive hernia. He did laugh about it, which I guess you could say is pretty strange, or testament to my comedy skills.

In 2003, I had one of my worst ever years. All four of my grandparents passed away in the space of twelve months. First, Oma and Opa left us. They were both in their nineties and died of old age. Then, in the summer, Nan and Granddad died within five weeks of each other. My granddad had a stroke and was taken to hospital; Mum took Nan in with us immediately. She would never have left either of them on their own.

Within a week of our taking Nan in, my granddad died, on 27 June. Sadly, he never even regained consciousness after the stroke. My mum kept her eye on Nan, but she knew something wasn't right. A doctor friend came by and he said, 'Let's take her into hospital to check her out.' She never came out again.

Mum wouldn't let them conduct a post mortem, so we don't have an exact cause of death – but we're convinced that Nan died because she and Granddad couldn't live without each other.

Their deaths hit us all hard. The events of the year really made me think about my life and what I wanted to achieve in it. Despite my almost constant stream of work, I still wasn't particularly satisfied with where my career was headed. Performing for punters in hotel bars and holiday resorts was all very well, and I was glad to entertain people, but it was hardly the big time.

Perhaps I needed to consider the small screen …

18

TV or not TV

I f you thought *I'd Do Anything* was my first TV appearance, you'd be very much mistaken. I've actually popped up on the box a fair few times over the years.

Trust me, though, I'm not one of those *Big Brother*-esque people who are desperate to become famous to get free entry into nightclubs and the chance to bonk a footballer. Rather, I'm a believer in living life to the full, and taking advantage of experiences that come your way. If the opportunity to appear on a TV show falls into your lap, why shouldn't you go for it?

Although my TV debut was on a Granada show called *A Taste For Travel*, in which Mum and I visited New York, my first proper TV experience was on Michael Barrymore's *My Kind of People*, back when I was eighteen or nineteen.

You probably remember the programme. It had two elements to it: a 'roadshow' that went to shopping centres around the country to film members of the public performing; and a studio-based music-themed game show, where you had to answer questions with a partner and do the odd bit of singing.

A bunch of us from Blackpool hired a coach and headed to the MetroCentre in Newcastle to see if we could get a spot on stage to show off our talents. I was with Dave and Carolyn – Gavin's parents – and that whole crowd. It was great fun.

As luck would have it, the producers gave me a shot to sing 'All That Jazz' from the musical *Chicago*. I went down a storm and Michael himself even came by to say he thought I was ace. I was well chuffed, let me tell you. To hear a man of his stature think that I was good put me on top of the world.

Little did I know that the best was yet to come. Just as we were about to get back on our coach, one of the researchers from the programme came up and told me that they'd like me to appear in the studio. I couldn't believe my ears. This was going to be my big break!

I was straight on the phone to Mum, who was thrilled – possibly mostly because she really loved Barrymore. Now, don't get me wrong: I was excited *not* because I was going to get my face on the telly, but because I was being given the chance to do what I loved – singing.

A few weeks later, my hairdresser Terry and I went on the show and took part in the quiz. I'd thought Terry might be good at the music questions, but we both sucked big time. Nevertheless, we had a blast. Just being in the studio and on a real TV set was so exciting for me. It was a whole new world, one that I was hungry for. I loved the energy and the buzz in the air. I knew this was what I wanted.

A short time later, I got another bite of the Barrymore cherry when Michael invited me to return for his last-ever show. He wanted some of his favourite contestants to come back and sing – and lucky old me was one of them. I was so honoured. When I sang 'Red, Red Wine', the performance came from the bottom of my heart.

In 2000, a producer, whom I had met on that first travel show I did with Mum, got in touch to see if I would be interested in appearing on Dale Winton's Saturday-night TV show at the time, *The Other Half*. I think once you've made contact with runners and researchers for these kinds of programmes and, crucially, made a positive impression, they remember you and want to invite you back for other projects, and they recommend you to their colleagues. That's certainly been my experience, anyway, and I've been really grateful for it.

The premise of *The Other Half* was that contestants had to guess who a celebrity's real spouse was from a line-up of three men or women. I had been chosen as a potential wife of Chris Eubank. For some reason, the wardrobe people dressed me up like an Indian woman with a bindi on my forehead, which was a bit confusing.

The recording was great, and I got to meet Jane McDonald and someone from Steps (the fella with the brown hair – Lee). Chris Eubank was a darling, if a little eccentric. Dale Winton, however, I could have just eaten up with a spoon. He is such a lovely guy. So good with people. So gentle.

After *The Other Half*, I was asked to appear on a New Year edition of *The Weakest Link*, which featured cabaret acts from across the country. I remember being a little bit nervous before going to the studio, because from what I had seen of the show, Anne Robinson always gave people a hard time.

She turned out to be a sweetie in the end, and was really nice to me. She even got me to sing, which I loved. In the end, I came fifth on the show. I was bumped off – quite rightly, too – after I got the question about who wrote Noddy wrong. For some reason, I had it in my head that it was Roald Dahl, when it was of course Enid Blyton. D'oh!

Next on my list was the 2005 series of *The X Factor*. Now, this one really meant something to me. I had watched the first series the previous year and had loved the fact that the contestants could actually *sing*. This was a show about finding talent, and with the legendary record producer Simon Cowell on board, I knew both the viewers and the music industry took it seriously.

By now, I was thoroughly fed up with doing the clubs. I wanted to break out of the cycle and find myself a proper career as a singer – yet I wanted it to last. I hoped *The X Factor* could give me that.

I rocked up to the Manchester audition feeling oddly nervous. This opportunity could give me a real chance of success. Sure, I'd appeared on *My Kind of People*, but that was a variety show where the public were given their chance to shine. *The X Factor* was different. This was a platform for people to demonstrate their vocal ability – or lack of.

While the previous year's winner, Steve Brookstein, had crashed and burned after the requisite post-show number-one single, the runners-up G4 had proved they had what it took to make it and were already selling albums by the bucketload. I wanted that. I wanted to build a career. I wanted longevity. I wasn't looking to get my face in the papers with two belts wrapped around my knockers. What I was after was to hear Simon Cowell say to me that I had a great voice and that I had the potential to go far.

After getting through two rounds of auditions with the show's researchers, I was told that I had made it through to see Simon, Sharon Osbourne and Louis Walsh. I was giddy. My dreams felt within reach at last.

When I stepped into the room, which was dressed with the programme's familiar logos, I was quaking. The judges on their podium were intimidating enough, but around twenty production crew were sitting to the left of the contestants' spot, too, making the experience even more nerve-racking.

Typically, one of my contact lenses slipped to the side of my eye as I edged into the room; I just hoped that they didn't think I had a nervous twitch as I tried discreetly to blink it back into place. I could feel sweat dripping down my back. Although I had played to much bigger crowds in the past, this performance meant so much to me.

'Come on, Jodie,' I told myself. 'You can do it.' And I knew I could. So, pulling myself together, I belted out a rousing Anastacia number, hoping it would be enough to put me through to the next round: the infamous boot camp.

I felt pleased with my performance. My voice had sounded strong and, in a good sign, the judges were smiling. Louis told me that I reminded him of a young Bette Midler, while

Sharon, who I must say had great skin (she also reminded me of my mum), told me she loved me. So far, so good. That left just Simon, a man who is notorious for never mincing his words. Would he like me as much as the others? His face was serious.

'I just don't get you,' he said. 'It's a no from me.'

Looking back, I'm guessing now that he perhaps saw me as another Michelle McManus, the large singer who won the 2003 series of *Pop Idol* – and promptly sank without a trace. Maybe he was scared to put me through after what had happened to her career. Luckily, his 'no' didn't make any difference, as Louis and Sharon had both given me a 'yes'. I was through to boot camp.

A short while later, the triumphant contestants were brought to London to be put through our paces at the Café de Paris nightclub. What surprised me was that there were *so* many talented people there, all battling to make it into the final four in our category, and go through to the live TV shows. What chance did I have? There were thinner, prettier people. Could I really compete with them?

On the first day, it was revealed who our mentor was going to be. Given Simon's comments at my audition, I hoped against hope that it wouldn't be him. If it was, I didn't stand a chance.

Fortunately, it was Mrs Sharon Osbourne who was in charge of my group, the over-25s. I was very pleased. Not only because I had always admired and respected her, but also because she reminded me of my mum, I also felt really comfortable in her presence and more able to keep my nerves under control.

I'd agonized over which song to sing at this stage of the competition. In the end, I opted for 'When I Fall In Love', the dreamy, powerful ballad recorded by Nat King Cole and Doris Day, among others. It was a decision that seemed to pay off, as Sharon gave me a warm smile when I'd finished my solo spot.

At boot camp, I met Brenda Edwards, who would go on to finish fourth in the competition. I don't know if I caught her on a bad day, but she didn't seem the friendliest person I have ever met. There was an empty seat next to her and I remember asking her if I could sit down; she gave me a withering look. I won't hold it against her, though, because it might just have been a tricky moment for her. I simply kept my distance.

The infamous Chico, who finished fifth, and eventual runner-up Andy Abraham were also there. Both of them were the loveliest guys you could meet – talented, too. They really deserved to get as far as they did.

I successfully made it through the first day's cut, which I felt was a massive achievement. Then, on day two, it came to the moment when we'd find out which seven contestants would go on to the 'judges' homes' part of the contest.

I wasn't sure which way my luck was going to fall. If I got through to the next stage, I would be ecstatic. If I didn't, I'd be disappointed, but I'd still be happy in the knowledge that I had got this far. After all, 75,000 people had auditioned.

I lined up on stage with four other contestants. Next to me was a right nutter, so I didn't hold out much hope. Sadly, the verdict wasn't positive – I was out of the competition. The good news was that Chico and Andy had survived the cull. Oh yeah, and so too had misery-guts Brenda. Oh well, *c'est la vie*.

Around the same time as the Manchester audition for *The X Factor*, I had my fingers in lots of pies. Nothing new for me there, I know – but this time, I wasn't eating them. One of my ventures was that I was trying out for a role in an upcoming production of *Hairspray* in London's West End. I was hot with anticipation about it because I thought the role of Tracy Turnblad was tailor-made for me. After all, she was the only fuller-figured West End leading lady.

The auditions were set out in two sections. I'd made it all the way down to the final four, and my ambition of playing a West End part felt just a few inches away from reality. Wretchedly, in the end it turned out that they couldn't bring over the set from Broadway for the London production, so we were all given the knockback and the show was put on hold.

This really broke the camel's back for me. After years of attending auditions for the West End, I'd been convinced that this was my moment. Yet it wasn't to be. A very kind man – who, little did I but know it then, would later play one of the biggest roles in my entire life – a marvellous man by the name of David Grindrod came over to say, 'Not this time, sweetheart.'

It really did crush me, that did; after that, I never auditioned for another West End job … till Nancy. I simply gave up hope. Sad to say, but I let go of my West End fantasy that day.

A while afterwards, I was approached in the street to take part in a Channel 4 documentary about a woman who was trying to put together a fat-girl beauty contest. I was at my heaviest at that point: 22 stone and a size twenty-six. At the extreme end of my obesity, I hated the way I looked, but, game for anything nonetheless, I went for an interview and met a lovely lady called Charlotte Coyle, a plus-size model. She told me that the idea behind the beauty pageant was to prove that larger women could be just as beautiful as thin people.

I liked the concept and thought it was fabulous that someone was standing up for the larger lady. I'd been big all my life and I had been made to feel inadequate at times. Finally, someone was defending that and saying, 'We're fat, take that, get used to it.'

The preparation for the pageant was tough. We were taught how to walk a runway, and there was a lot of focus on our own issues to do with weight, which I found difficult to discuss. I'd always had a laugh at my size, and made a habit of making jokes about it, but now I realized that I wasn't all that happy carrying around so many extra pounds. In fact, it made me feel sad. It got me thinking: if I was thinner, would life be better? Would my career take off? Would I find better men who would treat me right?

Fired up with enthusiasm, I began yet another diet. The beauty contest was for fat girls, but, let's face it, I was still going to be overweight for a long while yet, so I didn't have any worries about becoming too slim for my latest venture. Ha – I wished. But I thought that if I could lose a couple of stone, I might feel a little happier. I was pleased to drop a few dress sizes before the big day, which was something at least.

When the morning of the fashion show dawned, all the entrants were petrified, but we were also really excited and proud to be taking part in such a brave innovation. We strutted our stuff on the catwalk at the Café de Paris. It was strange to be back there after having experienced the *X Factor* boot camp in the very same venue. I could only hope for a better outcome this time.

We all waited with bated breath to find out which of us had impressed the judges enough to be crowned the pageant queen – and win a modelling contract with Marks & Spencer.

It turned out that it wasn't my turn to shine this time, and another girl won the prize. Unexpectedly, however, I was later approached by M&S to be their plus-size model. Unfortunately, I was told about the job just as I discovered that I'd made it on to a new series of LIVING's weight-loss TV show *Britain's Biggest Loser*, for which I had applied a few weeks before.

It was a dilemma indeed, as I couldn't do both. They were great opportunities and each could change my life. But which one would be the most beneficial?

In truth, I didn't have to think twice about which one I wanted the most. You always know, in your heart, what you really want out of life.

19

The Biggest Loser

For years, being fat was just a way of life for me. I had tried loads of diets, but they had never really worked long term. I'd sampled everything from the cabbage-soup diet (one time, the whole of the Prenger family were on that; if you have never tried it, all I'm going to say is that your house should have good ventilation) to the Heart Foundation plan, to diet pills that made me talk faster than if I'd downed thirty espressos ... I'd given them all a go.

Yet I never seemed able to make a fresh start of it. Each diet was doomed to failure even before it had begun. The KFC from the previous night always seemed to be in my gut, weighing me down and whispering that I could start tomorrow. Okay, so I'm a sham, but once you've fallen off the wagon, you might as well roll with it.

I didn't exercise properly, either. I tried every now and then, and one year my parents bought me a treadmill for Christmas – but I think Mum got more use out of it than I did. On Christmas Eve, she was standing on it as she put the finishing decorative touches to the machine as it sat under the tree. Dad wanted to check it worked, so he plugged it in and set it off. Mum, of course, immediately toppled over and fell in a heap on the floor, laughing her head off. Once it was unwrapped, I used it just a couple of times.

To be honest, because of my size, I've never felt right in

my own skin. Don't get me wrong, I've never felt clinically depressed or suicidal; I've just not felt right in myself. When I was growing up, adults and children would shamelessly call me fat, most of the time to my face. They'd say things like, 'How much did you weigh as a baby?' or 'I guess you don't care any more, you can eat what you like!' The cheekiness and blatant rudeness of these people really hurt me, but I developed a thick skin over the years and so I always tried to find the funny side.

Now in my mid twenties, I didn't want to sit back and just let life pass me by. These were supposed to be the best years of my life, but instead I was staying in, generally slumped on the sofa watching *Pretty Woman* to avoid skipping through 485 useless TV channels that I never watched anyway.

I was aware that the weight issue was starting to get to me. Physically, it was tiring me out. I was so weary from dragging my fat arse around the country; it was like carrying a couple of sacks of potatoes with me everywhere I went. It was exhausting. On a superficial level, I wanted to glance in the mirror and see a pretty, thin girl looking back. I wanted men to desire me. In addition, career-wise, I knew that if I wanted to get more work in the entertainment field, I really had to shed the pounds. After all, how many successful singers and actresses do you know who are over a size eighteen? And at this point, I was a size twenty-two.

I wasn't silly about it: I had no wish to become a size zero. That's just a stupid size; you can't tell me that anyone with that kind of figure is happy. All I wanted was to be able to walk through a door without bringing half the wall with me. My main problem was that, even though I was desperate to lose weight, I just didn't have the willpower to see it through.

Consequently, when I watched *The Biggest Loser* on TV and saw the miraculous results achieved by the contestants, I knew it was something I had to do. I remember so clearly sitting in front of the set with my mum and half a packet of HobNobs, watching the finale of the American series. I was stunned at how these people had totally transformed themselves. I didn't know then how long it had taken them or exactly how they'd done it, but what they had achieved brought me to tears. God, I am crying again now just thinking about them.

I recall looking over at my mum; I didn't even need to say anything. She saw in my eyes how I longed to be just like them, to lose what had been holding me back for years – and that was over a hundred pounds' worth of lard attached to my arse.

As I swept the biscuit crumbs from my jumper, I thought, 'Right, if they can do it, so can I.' Of course, if I'd had an English pound for every time I'd said that to myself before, I could have bought a small island.

Once the final credits had rolled, a voiceover announced that the show's producers were on the hunt for people in the UK who wanted to undergo a similar transformation. I had no hesitation whatsoever in putting myself forward: I had had enough of hiding sweet wrappers down the side of the sofa; I was fed up with food being the first thing I thought about when I woke up in the morning and the last thing I thought about when I went to bed at night. I couldn't handle it any more, I really couldn't. I'd reached the point where I was seriously considering having a gastric band. The advert for *Britain's Biggest Loser* felt like I was being thrown a lifeline.

The online application form was very detailed; so long and involved that I must have lost at least three pounds simply from using my fingers to fill it in. It covered everything: my early years, my eating habits, how much exercise I did, and so forth. It was hard to write down, though I have to admit that I did exaggerate a little bit by adding two extra cheeseburgers on to my food diary – just so they'd definitely get in touch.

I found the interview process, which came next, a breeze. Despite the fact that my curly hair extensions made me look like Ursula from *The Little Mermaid*, the producers could see that, behind the garish make-up and quip-filled banter, I was clearly unhappy about my weight. I told them that I had tried so many diets over the years, but that nothing had worked. I had to convince them that I needed to be put through a punishing regime in order to see results. The show was no holiday camp; there'd be no lying back and eating choccy digestives. I was prepared for blood, sweat and tears.

Before I received final confirmation as to whether or not my application was successful, I had to undergo medical and psychiatric evaluations, for safety reasons. I remember the doctor saying to me that he thought I'd be a great character for the programme, but that I stood no chance of winning – because a woman never could. Men lose weight faster than women, you see: that's a fact. His words were enough to fire me up. If that's what he thought, then I was determined to prove him wrong. I was now even more desperate to be the first female to win the series, if only to demonstrate that a woman could do it just as well as any man.

When I found out I had a place, I was overjoyed. I think Mum was a bit scared that I might go over the top in my desperation to lose weight, but I reassured her that this experience would be the making of Jodie Prenger.

Leaving home was tough. Mum must have known that I was in for a difficult time and I think she would have preferred it if I'd stayed at home and not pushed myself too hard. Yet I knew I had to do it; I needed to do it for me. I had been fat long enough. It was time to change my life.

The night before we entered the *Biggest Loser* house, all the contestants were sent to stay at various hotels in Somerset. The next day was the beginning of the rest of my life, I told myself, lying on my bed. So, I reckoned, it wouldn't matter if I said goodbye to my old life with a lovely slap-up meal.

I got the landlord of my hotel to drop me off at the local

pub. I felt like I was on death row. All I could think about was having a very tasty last meal – onion soup with lots of bread for starters, followed by a mean fillet steak with all the trimmings, then for dessert a mouth-watering hot fudge cake with ice cream. Oh yes, I had it all mapped out in my head.

I asked the landlord to pick me up in just sixty minutes, so there was no time to waste. As I waddled into the pub, every head turned my way. It was like that scene from *An American Werewolf in London*. I must have been the first new face most of them had seen since 1979.

As I looked at the curious faces staring back at me, no doubt judging me, the idea of sitting there in front of them all chomping down on my final feast was too much for me to bear. Instead of my dream meal, I opted for a bowl of mushroom soup with a single chunk of bread. In place of a chocolate fix, I had a Baileys coffee. Tantalizingly, the sumptuous smell of beef wafted across the pub and teased my nostrils.

'God,' I thought, 'what I'd do to get a gobful of meat.'

Having finished my not-exactly-filling soup, I realized I had fifteen minutes left before the landlord came to collect me. I had just enough time to call Mum. Wherever we were, there was no mobile signal, so I was told to try the phone box down the lane.

Stepping outside, I discovered that the booth was actually a little way from the pub, in a place where there were no street lamps. So as I tried to dial home, I could barely see which numbers I was punching in.

This was my final phone call to my folks: as from tomorrow, we were going to have to hand over our mobiles and cut off all contact with the outside world. Yep, that would mean no Internet, no TV, no newspapers, *nada*.

I cried as I came out of the phone booth: I hate saying goodbyes and never before had I gone more than a week without having any contact with my family.

The next morning, I woke up wondering what lay in store

for me. All I knew was that hopefully, in a matter of weeks, I could be half the woman I was now.

My first task was to move into a big luxurious house in the country, which belonged to the Duke of Somerset: the contestants' home for the duration of the series. It was very daunting. It felt like boarding school, only without all the home comforts, such as a secret stash of biscuits under the bed. Indeed, our handbags and luggage were searched on arrival so that not so much as a grain of sugar was allowed into the house. It was weight-loss boot camp at its best.

The house was practically in the middle of nowhere. You'd have to be a member of MFI – or is it MI5? – to find it. With the no-contact-with-the-outside-world rule in place, we were completely removed from our former lives.

The setting was amazing: a typical country mansion, filled with the most divine oil paintings you could imagine. The Duke of Somerset's family are descendants of Henry VIII and Jane Seymour, and there was a stunning portrait of the latter, which I just loved to look at from time to time. One of the bedrooms housed Henry VIII's very own bed: what a sight that was to see. Etched into the headboard was a drawing of a donkey having a fun time with a woman – how saucy!

One of the first things we had to do on camera was meet the fitness trainers, Angie Dowds and Mark Bailey. Naturally, as it was being filmed for TV, it wasn't just a case of shaking hands. It was a lot more dramatic than that: we came pounding over the hill to meet them. By the time we reached them, we were all sweating and out of breath.

After greeting us, the trainers made us do press-ups, some running and some crunches. Oh, dear Lord, what had I gotten myself into? On that first day, Angie said to us all, 'It's going to get worse than this. I don't care if I make you cry or make you sick.'

I have to admit, I seriously thought to myself, 'God, what have I done? I can't face any more of this.' But then my competitive streak kicked in. I remembered what I was there for and I was raring to go.

Second thoughts soon set in again, however, when the other contestants and I were put through the most humiliating experience ever: being weighed in front of each other and on camera.

To make it even more of a nightmare, we had to strip off and squeeze ourselves into swimming costumes for this main event. As you can imagine, it wasn't a pretty sight. Even now, I still find it hard to look back at myself. Not only did I resemble Nellie the Elephant, but you could also see right through my costume when the lights were on me – the cozzie went totally sheer.

Honestly, it was a tough thing to do: just to stand there in my bathing suit, with everyone looking at me, unable to hide the bits I'd normally keep covered. I was literally letting it all hang out. Anyone would find it hard, but I felt so uncomfortable standing there, more in the spotlight than ever – only this time, I didn't have a song with which to shield myself.

In truth, I felt ashamed that I had let myself get like that. We all stood there, like so many deers in the headlights, as we each stepped up on the scales. I remember making a joke about myself (typical Jodie); it was the only way I could deal with it. When I watch the episode back, I recognize the pain in my face: please God, may this be over – and quick.

I hated every minute of that day. Nevertheless, I knew it was the Jodie I wanted to say goodbye to. I didn't want to feel ashamed of myself; I didn't want to have to make gags about the way I looked to get by. I just wanted to be happy.

It turned out that I was one of the biggest of all the girls. That was tough to come to terms with. I'd never thought that in a camp for big people I would be among the heaviest. But no, at 18 stone 2 lb, I was tipping the top. When I saw that figure on the screen, I remember thinking to myself that I would never be that heavy ever again.

For those of you who never saw the programme, which aired on LIVING, I'd better describe the format of the show. First off, the twelve contestants were divided into two groups: initially, boys and girls. However, Angie Dowds said that she saw grit in me and thought it would be better if I joined the boys' team. I have to admit I felt like a right wally, being the only girl, but the fellas really took me under their wing.

In the end, I loved being in the guys' team. In some ways, I trained like a bloke, pushing myself as hard as they did. I constantly reminded myself that men lose weight quicker than women, so I had my work cut out for me. It wasn't easy. I remember one week Angie had us flipping tractor tyres, which wasn't a simple task with my acrylic nails. Nonetheless, I mucked in because I knew that that was what I had to do.

Each week, the teams would battle it out to see which of them could lose the most weight as a whole. The result wasn't determined by the number of pounds lost, but on the percentage of body weight lost. That's how you ultimately won the series as an individual, too – the winner wouldn't be the person who had lost the most weight per se, but whomever had lost the highest percentage of their body weight, calculated from what we'd weighed at the start.

The team with the smallest weight loss each week had to go into the elimination room, where you had to vote off a member of your own team. If ours was the losing team, we would immediately be separated so that we couldn't talk about who we wanted to send home.

Instead, we were asked to write down the name of the person on a yellow card, which would be placed under a service platter. That would then be opened in a dramatic 'reveal' come the moment of truth. We all knew it was part of the game and that we had to make that difficult choice, but nevertheless it was such a horrible experience to go through because you could see that by nominating someone you were destroying their dream.

The eliminations were undoubtedly the worst part of the whole experience. We were all there for the same reason: we all aspired to change our lives and lose the flab. To be kicked off before we had a chance to change for good would be a real blow to any of us. Of course, as the weeks progressed, it became even harder, as we then started having to vote off close friends.

I remember feeling absolutely dreadful when one of the contestants, Alan, got sent home. He was such a wonderful family man and I knew that he wanted to do well in the competition. In Alan's case, though, he had made it clear that he missed his family, so when it came to making my elimination decision, I tried to reassure myself that I was doing the right thing in choosing him.

Generally, I got on well with all the contestants – but especially with Alan, Andy, Amos, Ben and Lee, who are all just lovely.

Alan is a thoroughly decent man, while Andy is a real joker. It was great to find someone with the same sense of humour as me.

Amos is a fabulous gay chap, with whom I hit it off straight away. We had such a good laugh together. We were just like Bubbles Devere and Desiree from *Little Britain* – in fact, we used to swan around the house pretending to be them, squealing 'Darling!' at each other.

Ben is a total sweetheart; you couldn't help but love him. In fact, I just wanted to mother him. Over the course of the series, it was great to see his transformation.

Then there was Lee, who became my partner in the competition further down the line (five weeks in, the two teams were broken up and people divided into pairs instead). He is such a top geezer. He grew to be like a brother to me; we both went through so very much. When, in week eight, his girlfriend came to see us during the sole family visit we were allowed, I think she felt a little uncomfortable about how close we were. But nothing was ever going on; I wanted to tell her it was never like that. We could have slept naked and nothing would have happened. We were simply good support for each other.

In the first few weeks, we were given physical challenges and a whole new diet. It was hard to get used to – but we were aware that it was not only part of the programme, but also doing us some good. So we went along with it.

The physical challenges that we had to face were mind-blowingly tough. Sometimes, they would blindfold us so that we didn't know where we were going. And they were right to do that, because some tasks were so awful that you just didn't want to know what they had in store for us.

Our first challenge was pulling a fighter plane along a runway. Yes, you read that right: pulling a fighter jet. Who did they think we were – superheroes? Was it a bird? Was it a plane? No, it was Jodie almost doing herself a mischief trying to pull a plane. Somehow, though, I managed to get through it.

Every week before a challenge, we would have to visit the show's doctors, so they could make sure that we weren't damaging ourselves as we attempted to get fit. After all, we'd begun the programme being badly out of shape. To go suddenly from being a couch potato to someone who was really active was an extreme shock to the system, and there was a danger that we could do ourselves harm.

We were grateful to have the check-ups. The last thing any of us wanted was to be carted out of the mansion in an ambulance. Or worse: a massive wooden box. As the weeks progressed, it was amazing to watch how our blood pressure started to fall as we got healthier and healthier. We felt unstoppable, like the world was in our hands.

The challenges would take place on a Wednesday, with the all-important weigh-in the following day. The latter were always stressful, as you never knew how much weight you had lost. In fact, I could barely sleep on the nights before because I would worry about having gained weight or not losing enough. You'd only find out how much you currently weighed when you stepped into the room and, along with everyone else, saw your results come up on the screen.

We spent the rest of the week being put through our paces by Angie, or Superwoman as I liked to call her. Angie proved to be a really tough trainer. She kicked some welly all right. I was scared of her. She had this stern quality that could make people quake in their shoes.

Luckily, that's what I needed. If she had been soft with me, I probably would have become lazy and fallen off the wagon into a pit of chocolate biscuits, or just walked. But she made me work like I'd never worked before. She was hard as nails. She had to be, but I knew that there was a heart in there too. I saw her as a Cadbury's Creme Egg: she had a rock-solid exterior, but she was soft on the inside.

By the end of each day, I just wanted to crawl into bed and sleep. It was a gruelling regime: worse, probably, than being in the army. Nevertheless, we knew that even though the pain was killing us, our bodies were being worked to the core. I remember that I even found it hard to sit down on the loo; the muscles in my legs were that sore. It was such a comedy act. I look back now and laugh – what a sight that must have been.

Aside from the physical aspects of the regime, we were also taught to 'eat clean to get lean'. If we wanted to lose weight quickly and safely, it was the only way. That motto meant no sauces, no sugar, no butter and no cheese. Everything was cooked fresh. We weren't allowed carbs in the evening, and we had to make sure that we ate more than three hours before we went to bed, so as never to turn in with a full stomach.

We had a chef for the first week; then we were given individual food plans by the nutritionists, which we cooked for ourselves. I have to say that after only a short while, we'd learned so much about food that we didn't need the plans: we sorted our own food out. It was a bit like *Big Brother* in that we had to come up with a shopping list, but of course we had to choose the right foods.

I have to say, it was great. Gone were the days of my bacon butty in the morning, ham-and-cheese sandwich at lunch (with a packet of crisps and a Mars), and a Chinese takeaway for dinner. I went from noshing my bacon sarnie in the morning to enjoying fresh fruit and porridge. I tried lots of different foods – and not one of them a ready-made meal.

I was learning so much that it wasn't long before I started to cook for everyone like a mother hen. As a result, I began to love preparing food and now create my own recipes and devise healthy options all the time. Who'd have thought it, eh?

What I discovered was that there really is nothing you have to miss out on in order to get fit. There is always a pleasing alternative. You just have to be bothered to make the effort to create it. I also learned that portion control is a valuable tool: you only need to give your body as much as it needs. These days, if I want to snack, I'll have a few nuts or fruit – no more HobNobs for me.

As well as coping with the gruelling activities and the drastic change in diet, we had to adjust to being filmed around the clock. The cameras were there 24/7, getting you at your best times – and your worst.

We'd constantly be asked questions about our weight on camera, which was very difficult to deal with. I had never really talked to anyone about my size before, apart from my mum, so it really opened up the floodgates for me. It was so hard to discuss because I had to face some harsh truths. Nonetheless, I realized that it was the best thing for me to do.

Naturally, there were moments during the competition when I was low and thought I was wasting my time and the time of all the experts around me. I had a crisis of confidence one day and broke down in front of Angie. I was worried that I wasn't losing enough weight and that I couldn't keep up with the boys. Angie really got me through that week: she told me to find belief and I did, and that is what you have to do every day when you wake up.

Funnily enough, with no TV and no Internet, we all used to entertain ourselves by talking about food. We'd sit around and make ourselves hungry by discussing our favourite dishes. Well, what else was there to chew over? With talk of juicy Sunday lunches and tasty burgers, we made ourselves drool. It was torture.

In week five, the teams were dissolved into partnerships. I was with Lee, which I was very happy about because we got on so well. We proved to be a really strong team, both spurring each other on to do our best.

We used to get up at 5 a.m. and go out into the mansion's beautiful gardens, where we would swing that kettlebell and run circuits. We provided such a powerful support network for one another: when I felt like I didn't want to get up, he would push me, and the same would happen when he didn't want to get up; I would push him. Throughout it all, we stuck together.

One of our first joint physical challenges was one in which we were tied together and made to run down a hill; we then had to pick up loads of apples and press them to make apple juice. It was hard work, but we had a blast, mostly because we were working together and not against each other. We won that challenge and also won a juicer (freshly squeezed fruit juice, anyone?).

A week later, however, my enthusiasm was dealt a blow when we lost a rowing challenge. This was a trial where we had to row on rowing bikes in Bristol for three hours solid. I was the only person who didn't come off the rower once; I had that gut feeling throughout that I had the fire to see it through. Indeed, despite Lee and I losing out to Ben and his partner, who covered more miles, Angie said that she was impressed that I had given the challenge my all and had kept focused until the task was over.

Actually, that rowing challenge was an important moment for me in the series. It was a real turning point. The fact that I hadn't stopped once – not even to stretch my legs – and that I was the only contestant who had persevered with such commitment, made me think, 'If I can do this, I can do anything. I can go the extra mile. I can win.'

It wasn't all hard work. I celebrated my twenty-seventh birthday during my stay at the mansion. My family sent me the biggest bunch of balloons and flowers to let me know that they were thinking of me. The show's producers were wonderful too, throwing a party for me. Although there was no tasty cake on offer, we had a good time nonetheless – it was, in fact, just what we'd needed. We had been training with such focus that it was a relief finally to have a moment where we could all stop thinking about exercise.

During the party, we explored a bit more of the house. We had heard rumours that the old building was haunted. Frankly, I would have been disappointed if we hadn't. I'm not exactly a believer in ghosties and ghoulies, though, so I'd merely laughed off the suggestion that perhaps there was a lone spirit stomping the corridors, clanging its chains or slamming doors. But on this particular evening, I changed my whole belief system.

As a gift, the crew had bought me these tiny parachute things. A bunch of us ran upstairs to a balcony on the roof to throw them off, trying to hit the revellers below. As we made our way through the attic, the door slammed shut behind us, which made us all jump.

Of course, we were convinced at the time that it had just been the wind that had caused the door to shut so forcibly, and weren't unduly concerned. But when we went to head back to the party, we discovered that the door had been locked – twice over. I don't know what or who had turned that key, but I never went up to the attic again.

In time, my weight loss became noticeable. When I first entered the house, I weighed over 18 stone, so I was a whole lot of momma. As the weeks rolled by, I became determined to find the real me underneath all the layers of fat. I was adamant about shifting the weight. In the first week, I dropped to 17 stone 7 lb, a loss of 9 pounds. I then dropped another 5 pounds in week two. Week three saw me lose 4 pounds, and by week seven I was down to 15 stone 3 lb.

In week eight, we were all given a treat when our families surprised us with a visit. Up to this point, life in the house had been tough on the whole, as we had absolutely no contact with our loved ones, unless we were rewarded with the odd letter or video from home if we won a task.

Needless to say, I was thrilled to see my mum and dad. I had missed them so much and it was good to give them a hug and see that they were all right. Yet although I was pleased to be reunited with them, I didn't take my mind off my goal. I still needed to lose more weight; I couldn't be distracted. There was so much to lose – and I'm not just talking about the pounds.

By week nine, there were just three contestants battling it out to become Britain's Biggest Loser: Lee, Ben and me. The three of us had shed the most weight, but there was still a long way for us to go.

The next stage of the competition was to head back home and continue our fitness programmes there ... but without the help of our mentors.

20

Pretty Woman

Being cooped up in the *Biggest Loser* house had been like living in another world – being back in Blackpool with the smell of fish and chips and the rattle of crisp bags in the air was like torture. Nonetheless, I knew I couldn't be weak. I knew I had to stay strong and make sure I didn't slip. It was going to be hard, with all the temptations around me, but I was determined not to muck everything up at the final hurdle.

At home, I made sure I was eating the right things, like chicken, vegetables, salad and fish. I also continued to do the cardiovascular workouts Angie had taught us. And I stuck to it. I worked myself like a dog. After all, I had something to prove – not just to myself, but to Angie and my family, and to all those people who had made a joke about me being fat.

Being home again was weird. My mum and dad had tears in their eyes when they saw me for the first time, and couldn't believe the way I looked. Even my brother Marko, who had put on a bit of weight himself, was stunned by my shocking transformation – so much so that he would later be inspired by my hard work and shed loads of weight of his own.

And Ryan. Remember him? The Waterfront drummer I was madly in love with once upon a time? Well, he couldn't believe his eyes either when he saw me. But more about him later.

Upon leaving the *Biggest Loser* house for the home stage of the contest, we were all given a year's membership to Fitness First gyms. It was at my local branch that I met two very dear friends, Inny and Saj. Inny is a boxer and it was through going to boxing classes that we all became pals. Saj is my boxing buddy – I tell you that girl can bag a punch.

To stop me getting lazy, in addition to my Fitness First sessions I also called upon the services of ex-army tough man John Aberdeen, who made sure I worked hard. Saj, Inny and John played such a crucial part in my weight loss. It would take a lifetime of gratitude to thank them for what they have done.

Partly because of their friendship, training for me became like a religion. I trained every single day without fail. I was up jogging in the morning; I would always go for a run with John in the afternoon; then at night-time I would pop to the gym for a boxing class, rpm (spinning but better, I say), or a danceasize. I had to stay really focused – because the main thing I'd learned was that all the fad diets in the world don't work when it comes to losing weight. Trust me, I know. The only way to do it is to eat clean and train hard. You have to keep at it and stay committed, no matter what.

There were always going to be days when I wanted to reach for a Mars bar, and I had plenty of them to say the least. Yet it was during those moments when I felt at my weakest that I had to be at my strongest, and kick those cravings into touch. I would ask myself: was it a need or a greed? And for the most part, it was a greed.

I had another trick to help me, too. When I first went into the house, Angie told me to write down five reasons why I was there, not to give them to anyone, but just to remind me, every day, why I was doing it. I still have that list today, which I've never shown anyone, but its very existence helped me and spurred me on.

Yet for every up, there is a down. You see, with the structured diet and focused training, I pushed myself to the limit. I'm ashamed to admit that I became slightly obsessed. I remember thinking, 'Just thirty more minutes on the treadmill,' when I had already trained for three hours that day. Or I would put a morsel of food into my mouth and then spit it out, reasoning, 'I can't eat that, it will make me put on weight.'

All in all, I really have been through it when it comes to body size: I've seen both ends of the stick, as it were. So although I felt as thin as a rake going back to the *Biggest Loser* house for the final – after three months of hard graft at home – I also felt very weak at the same time.

All the contestants returned for the final weigh-in. I remember that night so clearly. Before I left my room that evening, I took a moment to look at myself in the mirror. I was wearing a black Karen Millen dress that I had bought from eBay especially for the occasion, and it fitted me like a glove. Staring at my reflection, I couldn't believe it was the same Jodie Prenger who had stepped on those scales all those months before, looking like the bloody Hindenburg.

It was a totally different me. Did I know this person who was blinking back at me? I had never been thin before, I had never seen my ribs; the only ribs I knew were the ones that came loaded with BBQ sauce at TGI Fridays. I almost didn't recognize myself.

That might sound a silly thing to say, but once you get used to a big girl staring back at you in the mirror, you just see that as you, regardless of how much you actually weigh. It's weird: even though I was now a size ten, I still thought of myself as being a large person. It takes such a long time to adapt.

I always say with weight loss that people think it's all about the food – and it's not. A lot of it is mental: there is so much you have to readjust in your life.

As I made my way to the final, I was almost sick with nerves, because I'd spent the past few months working myself to the max. At this stage, I thought I would only be happy with a win. Otherwise, I feared I'd feel like I had just been wasting my time. In reality, of course, whether I came first, second or third, I had still managed to shift an incredible amount of weight – and I looked fantastic in my designer dress. With my new figure, I was a winner, whatever the result.

When we arrived at the house for the recording of the show, none of us were allowed to see each other. I wasn't even able to see Angie, with whom I was most eager to catch up. Yet I knew that the 'reveal' was going to be the most spine-tingling moment in the entire series, so I was willing to sit tight just a little bit longer.

Waiting backstage, I could hear the cheers for Lee and Ben as they took their turns to show off their new physiques. I was so glad that I was in the final with those guys. They had been lovely and they really deserved to be there. Nevertheless, in my heart I wanted to be Britain's Biggest Loser – and as much as I loved those boys, I was hoping they didn't stand a chance of winning.

When the producers put me behind the paper screen I was to burst through for my 'reveal', I felt nervous and excited: nervous, because a lot was riding on this moment, and excited because I couldn't wait to show everyone the new me. Watching myself back on the telly, I'm still amazed by my silhouette on the screen. I look so thin. I can't actually think of that person as me … but it was.

As I burst through the screen, the gasps from the studio were clear. Angie looked winded, tears filled the eyes of the other contestants and I could see Ben mouth the words, 'Oh my God!' They were all so stunned by my transformation. They just couldn't believe their eyes.

Trust me, I adored the reaction. I was so pleased that after all the hard work, I had managed to surprise so many people. Seeing Angie's totally dumbstruck face was priceless. It was worth every gruelling challenge she'd put me through.

Then I took in the appearances of my fellow competitors. It was so good to see them again. Both boys looked great and had visibly lost a shedload of weight. But had they lost more than me? We were about to find out.

Ben was up first. At the start of the competition, he had weighed in at 20 stone 10 lb. Tonight, six months on, he was 14 stone 9 lb: he'd lost almost a third of his body weight. He looked ecstatic and I was so proud of him.

Lee was on the scales next. The digits showed that, since the show had begun, he had lost a whopping 10 stone 6 lb. His achievement meant the pressure was on.

Now it was my turn: the moment of truth. My hands were clammy, sweat was beading on my forehead, and my feet were aching. It was beyond tense. Yet even before I stepped on those scales, I felt like I had already won. At long last, I was the person I'd always wanted to be. The question was: had I lost enough weight to win the competition?

I stepped up on the scales. On the big screen behind me, my original weight figure began to tumble. All those months ago, I had started the show at a hefty 18 stone 2 lb. Now, after all the hard work, hard graft and tears, I was 9 stone 9 lb: a massive loss of 8 stone 7 lb ... 46.9 per cent of my total body weight. I had won. It was the most enthralling, bizarre experience of my life. I had gone from a dress size twenty-two down to a ten. I couldn't believe that this was me. I had won the competition, and £25,000 to boot.

It was Angie I had to thank for it. Yes, I had done the actual training. But without her drilling into me what I needed to do, I would never have succeeded. I owed her so much – for helping me lose the weight, and for giving me a second chance.

I was so grateful to Angie that I wrote a testimonial for her website. The words sum up everything I have to thank her for:

This woman has given me back my life, made me believe in myself and taken my fitness to a level I just didn't think it could go to. I may sound dramatic – well, okay, I am a bit of a drama queen – but seriously, Angie saved my life. I resigned myself to being overweight and unhappy for the rest of my life, but Angie dragged me straight out of my rut with her 'no-nonsense, get-the-job-done' approach. Not only that, Angie gave me the tools and the strength to become the first woman in the world to win *The Biggest Loser* TV show. I see Angie as the best – and such an amazing person at the same time.

Back at home, I was chuffed to be able to give away some of my outsized clothes to charity shops (and passing circuses).

At first, I found it odd to wear garments in which my legs didn't rub. But the biggest change of all was the joy I felt on hitting the high street, on a mission to buy the kind of clothes I'd always wanted to wear. Now, the shop assistants didn't look at me as if I had made a mistake walking into their boutiques, knowing at a glance that I'd never fit into any of their stock. I felt just like Julia Roberts in *Pretty Woman* – only I wasn't a whore.

I will always remember buying my first pair of jeans in Primark with my mum. I bawled my eyes out. I could never wear them before because my legs were too big.

Even though I was keen to replace my wardrobe, I did hang on to a few choice items, just to remember how I used to be. I know I've said I was ashamed of myself, and I was, but in some ways I'm also glad that I was a large girl and had to struggle. I think everyone takes a journey in life that makes them who they are. Losing weight was something I had to do. It's made me the person I am today – not just on the outside, but on the inside too.

My new way of life wasn't as easy as I anticipated it would be, though. With my super-slim figure, I thought I was invincible. I thought I could eat anything I wanted; that the weight wouldn't go back on. But it does, it creeps right back on to your hips.

Today, I am not the weight I was when I won *The Biggest Loser*. The difference is that I have learned from my mistakes and I now have the knowledge of how to lose weight if I want to. I'm back at the gym and I'm eating well, enjoying things like chicken and a salad, or fish or prawns.

Looking back, I think I spent so much time concentrating on losing weight that I wasn't prepared to be thin. I lost almost 9 stone in six months. That's pretty fast by anyone's standards. You feel totally different, and you have a lot to adjust to and change.

What was really weird for me was that people treated me differently, especially men. In all honesty, I felt kind of angry about that. I thought to myself, 'Yeah, *now* you want to talk to me. I was just the same person when I was bigger.'

I hate that in people. My experience is a reflection of the sad, material world we live in. It shouldn't be like that. Whatever size you are, you are the same person inside. I say that the thing that makes people beautiful in the first place is their imperfections. I wasn't trying to be perfect when I lost the weight. I wanted my health back, and I wanted to fit into a pair of jeans and feel good about myself.

As amazing as I looked at my thinnest, I don't think I would ever go back to being as skinny as I was at the end of *The Biggest Loser* – from choice. I simply didn't feel 'all woman'. I believe that women should be proud to have curves and to be shapely. I hate all this size-zero malarkey. The secret is to eat well and keep fit and that way you will maintain a healthy body. Most importantly, I think it is essential to feel comfortable in your own frame. At 9 stone, I felt too thin. I didn't feel like me. Now a stone or so heavier, I feel a lot better.

Don't get me wrong: I never want to be as big as I once was again, although the temptation to eat is always there. I love food, I love going out with friends. I never get these people who say, 'Oh, I forgot to eat lunch.' Usually after I have had my brekkie, I'm thinking about what I might have for my midday meal. I simply don't strive to be super-skinny. Life's too short and I am happy the way I am.

I know that many people aspire to lose weight. To anyone out there who might be inspired by my story, I would say that there is really only one certainty when it comes to weight loss, and it's that everyone's journey is unique. What works for one person might not work for another.

If you want advice, though, what I can say is, if you really want to make that change, then you have to take that first step. You have to go out there and do it, and not just say the words, 'I will start tomorrow.' Do it now, do it tonight. If you're sat on the sofa reading this book, put it down for five minutes and go for a jog around your neighbourhood, or join a gym. Your time is always what you make it, and you are the only person who can make that change.

Trust me when I say it'll be worth it in the long run. I know first-hand how unhappy sitting there fretting about the size of your bum or thighs can make you feel. I realize it's the first thing you think about in the morning and the last thing you think about when you go to bed. I waited long enough for the weight-loss fairy to come and wave her magic wand and she never bloody did. You just have to get off your backside and do it yourself.

21

Be Careful What You Wish For

As you can imagine, winning *Britain's Biggest Loser* changed my life completely, in many ways. Not only was my body totally different, but my mind and outlook on life altered too. There were also two other, very unexpected, changes that took place as a direct result of my time on the show.

First off, it was financially rewarding. In all honesty, and I'm not just saying this, the money part of the programme had never really appealed to me. In fact, it never even crossed my mind. Of course I'm not so rich that I can turn my nose up at a handout of twenty-five grand, but my reasons for taking part were so not about that. I really did want to change my body, change my life. The money was simply a rather nice bonus.

Afterwards, I had to think long and hard about what to do with the cash, as I'd never planned for the windfall. Should I refill my wardrobe with smaller-sized clothes? Or take myself off on a sun-soaked holiday and flash my new bikini body? Perhaps I should celebrate my win by stocking up on twenty-five-grand's worth of chocolate cakes and getting fat again? Never!

In the end, I decided that I wanted the money to do some good and provide people with the kind of life-changing experience that the TV show had been for me. I wanted to give something back. The idea I came up with was to set up a series of 'weight-loss weekenders'.

Basically, they were getaways for anyone who needed some guidance – for people who had reached the end of their tether and wanted to do something about their battle with the bulge. The weekenders included advice on diet and training, and there was a chance to talk about the reasons people had let the weight build up. I wanted to share everything that I'd been taught on *The Biggest Loser* with those who now found themselves in the same position that I had been in, before I was lucky enough to take part in the show. My old friend Angie Dowds and I ran the weekends together: Angie imparted her exercise expertise, while I took on the role of agony aunt.

It didn't take long for word to get around, and I was pleased that people thought the idea was useful. One of the women who signed up for a weekend was Samantha Haysom, the sister of a friend I used to go to school with.

On the surface, Sam seemed settled and happy, with a loving husband and children, but deep down she was mentally scarred from a vicious sexual attack that had taken place back in 2002. Thereafter, she became a recluse, became depressed and put on weight. She later suffered a stroke and developed epilepsy.

She had told me that her life had changed drastically and that she felt she was no longer living a real life: she was just existing, going through the motions of every day. As a result, she felt like she was neglecting her husband and children, by not being the person she was before the attack.

Sam signed up for one of my weekends, and came away afterwards feeling refreshed and revitalized. Of course, she still had anxieties. I wasn't offering a magical cure. Nevertheless, I like to think that getting away and talking through things helped to make her life a little easier to deal with.

I was so flattered when, in an interview with the *Blackpool Gazette* during *I'd Do Anything*, she said that I *had* helped her to get her life back on track in some way. She was a real sweetheart to give the interview, as her reasons for doing so were to show the world another side of me. I'd been portrayed a bit as a fun-seeking, brash northern Nancy on the programme, but Sam wanted people to know that, in her opinion, I had a heart of gold.

'Jodie made me want to live again,' she told the paper. 'She helped me to release the pain that had built up inside, she gave up her time to help me become myself again. I can never thank her enough. It may sound dramatic, but Jodie gave my children their mum back, my husband his wife, and my family the old Sam.'

When I read that, I cried my heart out. I found her words so moving. If I am in any way responsible for any of that ... In my opinion, no one deserves to be alone and unhappy. No one should live in the shadow of any sort of fear. We have one life to live: there is no point in letting it drift past us without making the most of every moment.

I didn't put on my weekends to be seen as some kind of saint. I staged them because I have had bad times in my life when it would have been nice to have someone to turn to. We all have problems; no one is perfect. Yet in many cases, problems can be solved just by talking about them, or by trying to make the most of what life has to offer. It may sound very 'Disney' and hippy trippy, but that's my philosophy.

The other thing to come out of my *Biggest Loser* win was the sudden change in my relationship with Ryan, the Waterfront drummer. Now, as I've mentioned before, we'd been great friends ever since college. Although I was dating his band mate, Mark, for a time, it was Ryan that I secretly loved. He was funny and handsome and all I could want in a guy ... except that he didn't fancy me. Sure, we'd had a few tipsy snogs every now and again over the years, but that was as far as it went. He just didn't want anything else from me.

Nevertheless, we were always there for each other and, eventually, went into business together: just before I entered the *Biggest Loser* house, we set up an online store called Rumpys that sold novelty buckets. Now, they weren't just any sorts of bucket. We lived in Blackpool, after all – and with the huge amount of hen and stag dos that take place there, what better gift for the hen or stag than to give them a hen bucket, stag bucket, kinky or love bucket? You know the kind of thing. We also sold fluffy handcuffs, vibrators – various items you might find on a hen or stag do: all rather innocent stuff, nothing sleazy.

I went off to do the show and left Ryan looking after the business. It was funny, but even though years had passed, I still harboured feelings for Ryan. In fact, I think part of the reason I was so keen to lose weight on *The Biggest Loser* was so that I could try to make Ryan fall for me. Although he had never said as much, I was guessing that the reason he'd never fancied me was because I was larger than life. It was a long shot, but I thought that if I came back looking completely different, there might be a chance that he'd change his mind about me.

Of course, that was just a small thing in my mind. The main reason I wanted to lose weight was for me. I wanted my life to change so that I could be happy, and not just so that some boy would suddenly find me attractive. If that had been my goal, I doubt I'd have found the courage and the willpower to stick to my guns.

When I came home from the *Biggest Loser* house, before the final weigh-in, I was nervous. Over the past few months, I had transformed considerably. It was a weird feeling to be heading back to the people I loved, because I felt like such a different person. I wasn't sure how everyone would react.

When I turned up at Mum's house, I found my family

and friends in the garden waiting for me. They were stunned by my drastic new appearance. I was naturally curious to see what Ryan thought of me ... and I wasn't disappointed. When he laid eyes on me, his mouth almost hit the floor. I could tell that he was impressed and all of a sudden I could see a burning passion in his eyes. Without blowing my own trumpet too much, I could tell that he fancied me.

'You look great,' he told me, running his eyes over my new svelte body. 'You look really great!'

I couldn't believe that, after all these years, Ryan finally found me attractive. Losing weight had done so much for me. I had a brand new body that I adored, and I had managed to win the heart of the man I had loved for almost a decade.

We started dating straight away. I was in ecstasy, floating on a cloud of love. This was what I had been waiting for for so long. I couldn't be happier. Ryan seemed pretty chuffed to be with me, too.

It was a wonderful time. I had gained so much confidence from being on the show that I could walk with my head held high, and for the first time I felt sexy, a woman who could be desired. In the past, I wouldn't catch people's eyes because I wouldn't want them to notice me (not that it was difficult to see me, being as I was the size of a Pontin's chalet).

I remember, when I was at my heaviest, that I was always aware that people were sniggering at me. Everyone laughs at the fat bird. I guess I made it easy for them, too, by wearing hair extensions that made me look like Vanessa Feltz, having long nails and sporting the brightest, most garish outfits. But now I could walk down the street and know that whenever someone looked at me, they weren't able to tease me about my size. That was a relief. It meant I could go anywhere, at any time, and not be conscious of people leaning over to the next person and saying something about my fat arse. It was liberating, it really was.

Shedding that 8 stone made me feel like I had come out

of hiding. Finally, people could see the real me. I wasn't ashamed of myself any more: I was proud to be Jodie. I didn't care if people looked at me – because now I knew that they weren't laughing and pointing at me any more.

I felt like my life had started at long last. After decades of living in some kind of cocoon, things were falling into place. For years, I had wanted to find love, but had always found the door slammed in my face instead. Yet now I had found what I'd been looking for – and with the very person I had hoped would give it to me.

I can't explain how excited I was to be with Ryan. Sometimes, I used to think that this must all be a dream, like the ones I'd had back at college when I'd first met him. After all, how often do people end up with the boys they used to love from afar?

Now, I know what you're thinking. It all sounds too good to be true. And you'd be right. As you can tell from my life, just as everything appears to be going well, something happens that brings my world crashing down around me. And that something came along all too soon.

Ryan and I were driving down the motorway one day. I wanted to know if the only reason for the years of small knockbacks from him, of him never inviting me out with his other mates, of him and I never getting together, *was* because he thought I was too fat. Bracing myself, I asked him outright.

His answer wasn't what I expected. He said, all matter-of-factly, 'Yes, that's right.'

In that instant, everything changed. I felt like the ground had gone from under my feet. It was at that moment that my feelings for him changed. Even though I'd probably known in my heart that Ryan was going out with me now only because I looked so different, I had kind of hoped that he had always loved me and just hadn't shown it.

But those few words were enough to destroy the burgeoning

relationship we shared. I couldn't go out with a man who was with me for superficial reasons. I wanted someone who loved me whether I was 8 stone or 50 stone. Ryan, it turned out, just wasn't that man.

After that, I went cold, and although we continued to date for a while, it was clear that I wasn't as into him. My feelings had literally flicked off like a light switch. Of course, he sensed that something was wrong. Sometimes, I wouldn't take his calls because I just couldn't bring myself to talk to him. It was messy for a long time, for various reasons that I won't go into here, but what we had was well and truly over.

A few years later, when I was appearing in *I'd Do Anything*, Ryan crept out of the woodwork again and sold a couple of stories on me. I had to complain to the Press Complaints Commission that Ryan's comments were inaccurate and intrusive. The complaint was resolved when the newspaper concerned removed the article from its database and undertook not to repeat any of the disputed points.

I guess that's the downside of fame. I'm nowhere near as famous as Victoria Beckham or Cheryl Cole, but that doesn't stop people trying to sell a story about me, whether or not it's true. It amazes me that people are allowed to go to a tabloid and give them some cock and bull story and get it printed. It's shocking. It hurts not just the person involved, but their family too.

Now, as I am starting to make a name for myself, I worry about what people can do to me. All I have ever wanted was to entertain. Yet sometimes, doing the thing I love most can bring so much heartache.

22

I'd Do Anything

It was my mum who told me about *I'd Do Anything*. She'd heard about it on the radio and said to me, 'Jodie, it's perfect for you.'

I wasn't convinced. I'd had so many knockbacks for West End work in the past that I wasn't sure if I could put myself through it all over again. At that stage, in January 2008, I was going through a phase when I'd kind of given up on singing. I felt like I was getting nowhere with it. I kept my hand in every now and again and did the odd show at the Mardi Gras or at Blackpool Pride, but my heart wasn't in it any more. I had become disillusioned.

Despite my initial reservations, the idea behind *I'd Do Anything* definitely appealed to me. I loved the musical *Oliver!* and secretly thought I was the perfect person for Nancy, the tart with a heart. But would I be good enough to make it? I'd come close with *The X Factor* three years before – would I do any better now? And did I really have the strength to put myself through yet another TV series?

In 2007, I'd watched the BBC's previous talent search, *Any Dream Will Do*, in which Andrew Lloyd Webber had found a new Joseph in the gorgeous Lee Mead, and had loved it. With Graham Norton hosting, and Denise Van Outen and John Barrowman on the judging panel, it was must-watch Saturday night TV.

The best thing was, like *The X Factor*, it was seeking proper talent. In fact, the show was better than its rival because it dispensed with the novelty auditionees and really focused on those performers who had what it took. In the end, that's what convinced me that taking part in *I'd Do Anything* would be a good thing.

I knew I had a strong voice and there was no doubt that I could command a stage, so in some ways I thought I was a shoo-in. That sounds big-headed, but it's not. Really. I know my strengths and I know my weaknesses. And if I'm good at one thing, it's singing. Entertaining people.

So, without any further hesitation, I sent off an application form, and was asked to an audition in Manchester. I turned up in a lovely red dress I had bought in a sale at River Island, hoping to stand out from the crowd. It was just as well my clothes were striking, for the audition was like a cattle market – there were so many people there, all with stars in their eyes.

Some were practising in the queue or in the loos, and I was surprised to hear that a lot of the hopefuls were very good singers. When I'd auditioned for *The X Factor*, I remember that while there were a handful of really great vocalists, most of those who had turned up looked totally ridiculous or sounded just terrible. But it was clear that the majority of the girls who had turned out for the Nancy auditions were serious contenders.

To start with, we were divided into groups of ten and asked to sing 'It's A Fine Life' or 'Oom-Pah-Pah'. Of the group I was in, only two girls went on to the next round, so I knew it was going to be tough.

I was one of the lucky ones, and made it through to see one Mr David Grindrod for a filmed audition. You may remember me mentioning him earlier in this book: he was the guy who auditioned me for *Hairspray*. I never thought I would cross paths with him again.

When my name was called to go through to perform my solo song, I felt a little nervous, but not as badly as I had done in the past. I think having auditioned so many times before, I'd become used to the pressure and I didn't feel as terrified as I might once have done.

In addition, I was feeling a lot more confident generally. When I had tried out for *The X Factor*, I was twice the size and, let's face it, never really in the running to win. Now, I had shed so much weight and gained so much self-assurance that I felt I was invincible, that I could do anything in the world. So when I sang in front of the cameras, I wasn't as self-conscious as I once would have been. For a start, I didn't have to worry about the extra ten pounds that the camera puts on you.

Having said that, when I watch my first audition tape again, I wonder what the hell I was doing with my face. With my lips sticking unattractively to my teeth, I have seen better heads on a witch doctor's belt. Not only was my face doing odd things during my performance, but I also began off-key. I had to ask the pianist to start over with a different song: never a great thing to do at an audition, but I just had to.

Mercifully, I managed to impress David with my singing. My lively performance of 'Don't Rain On My Parade', my second song, was good enough to send me through to the next round. When David told me that they wanted me to come back, he compared me to a pack of wild horses – and Faith Brown. I was happy to be compared to anything. My foot was in the door.

The next stage of the competition was another audition a few weeks later, this time in a studio. The number of girls had been slashed yet again. We were told that we had to sing in front of John Barrowman, Denise Van Outen and David, as well as an audience of the contestants' friends and family.

I brought Steve, the new guy I had just started going out with, along with me, and he sat proudly in the front row.

I had met him a few weeks before on a website and we had hit it off really well. In fact, our relationship was going so smoothly that I thought perhaps this one was a keeper.

When it came to my turn to perform, I was more excited than scared, and was feeling as sparky as hell. I was so thrilled to be there and felt so at home on the studio floor that I was smiling from ear to ear. John told me to kick off my shoes, which I did. They flew right across the studio ... and then I died a thousand deaths when I saw them land sole side up.

You see, in the preceding days, I'd gone shopping for a new outfit for the latest audition. River Island had come up trumps again on the clothes, and I was wearing a striped humbug pencil skirt with a coordinating top. After purchasing that combo, I'd tottered into New Look to browse for accessories. The shoes in question had matched my outfit perfectly, and I was pleased to have snapped them up for the bargain price of a fiver.

But, when I tossed them over to the other side of the studio, those big £5 stickers on the soles were as clear as day to everyone. Fortunately, I don't think the panel could see me blush under the inch of make-up I had on.

Before I sang a note, John started chatting to me about my relationship with Steve, and I told him that this audition was actually our seventh date – and that our third had been at the Manchester try-outs. My bubbly nature seemed to appeal to John; he loved everything I said and was in hysterics for most of our conversation. He even banged his hand on the table to stop himself from laughing, and then he said, 'Stop the boys talking, and sing ...'

Off I went, trilling like a bird in a tree, but almost as soon as I'd started – or so it seemed – John held up his hand to signal me to stop. At first, I was a bit concerned that he had cut me off in my prime, but then I could tell from John's smiling face that all was well.

'I have not laughed that way for so long,' he said, referring to our conversation and not my singing. 'You have had some drama experience. But is it enough?'

He let the question hang in the air for a moment, no doubt to create some televisual tension. It worked; my heart quaked. Then he finally put me out of my misery.

'Jodie ... You are going to Nancy School.'

Wow! I was through! I was overjoyed. As I dashed backstage, Graham Norton pulled me over for an interview and persuaded me to call my mum at home to tell her that I had made it to the next round.

While I was screaming down the line at her, the Lord himself, Andrew Lloyd Webber, strolled up. I was gob-smacked. 'Oh my God, it's him,' I gasped.

He must have thought I was a right numpty. The thing with Andrew is that he is a shy man, so I wouldn't be surprised if he'd thought I was some kind of madwoman when he first met me. Nevertheless, he is such a gentleman that he was very polite, even if he did look a little scared.

At Nancy School, the pressure really kicked in. When I arrived at the studio, which was a huge old school building in the heart of London, I realized just how privileged I was. Ten thousand girls had auditioned ... now just forty-eight remained. Boosted by John Barrowman's positive comments, I felt confident about the competition and truly believed I stood a chance of making it to the live finals.

Yet I hadn't anticipated how hard the competition was going to get. I was thrown in at the deep end, big time. Half the girls were fresh out of drama school. Some had already had a taste of life on the West End stage. Then there was me, who hadn't had anywhere near as much theatrical experience. But even though I hadn't treaded the boards in a big show, I knew in my heart that I was doing the right thing. This was a unique opportunity to do something I had always wanted to.

On our first day, we were told to remove all our make-up, so we could strip away all our outer layers and be raw and feel from the heart. I had no problem with that, but some of the girls found it absolutely devastating. That was the first test.

For the next few days, we were put through the wringer by singing coaches Claire and Donna, and Kevan the choreographer. It was hard work: the BBC had us training with the best in the business. I relished the chance they were giving me. Each night, we were all exhausted and relieved to head back to our hotel.

I roomed with a girl called Helen French. We got on wonderfully. We had loads in common and she was always up for a laugh. We'd be there of a night doing our fake tan, painting our nails – I even let her see me in my curlers.

Our days were long, but they had to be: whoever won would be putting on an all-singing, all-dancing show, six times a week. Looking back now, it amazes me how we did it, launching straight into that intensive process. Talk about 0 to 60 in 6 seconds!

During the week, we took parts from *Oliver!* and had to act them out. I remember that Andrew Lloyd Webber popped in one day to have a listen, which was incredibly nerve-racking. As ever, he was supportive and very kind, but my heart was pounding away like mad as he watched us work.

When it came to the cut on the last day, we were put into pairs and asked to rehearse either 'On My Own' from *Les Mis*, or 'Not That Girl' from *Wicked*. It was then down to Donna, Claire, Kevan, Denise and John to decide which of us had what it took to stay in the competition.

I sang 'Not That Girl', and hoped I had done enough to get through to the final eighteen. We'd all worked our hardest and sung our hearts out, so this last cull was excruciating. To make matters worse, it was announced that we would find out our fate through a nail-biting elimination process.

All of us were gathered together and told to sing once more. During the song, John would identify the unlucky ones by walking amongst the girls. If he tapped you on the shoulder, you were out; if you remained singing by the end, then you were through.

I'm not lying when I say the next few minutes were the most tense of my life. The song in question was 'As Long As He Needs Me'. We were instructed to perform it on a loop – but every time we started over, we all seemed to go a key higher. It was like *Oliver! The Opera* by the end.

Staring straight ahead of me, I sang with guts. In the corner of my eye, I could see John circulating the room and tapping girls on the shoulder. At one point, he walked past me, and I sensed him hovering behind me. Was my luck about to run out?

Happily: no. I was one of the lucky ones. I was set to go to Lord Lloyd-Webber's estate, Sydmonton, to continue my fight for a place in the live finals. It was at this stage that we had to perform at Andrew's private theatre, in front of a very special audience, which would include stars such as Barbara Windsor.

Andrew's mansion was amazing, set in the most stunning grounds. John Barrowman described it as 'fabulous, fabulous, fabulous,' and he was dead right. It was a lovely fancy pile, the like of which I had never seen before. The *Biggest Loser* house just paled in comparison.

When you strolled through the rooms, you couldn't help but notice all of Andrew's awards lying around. He even had an Oscar sitting there, which I was very impressed by. He wasn't showing off or anything – he's won so many accolades, where else is he to put them but around his house?

It was somewhat intimidating, though. Here I was in the house of a genius. And who the hell was I? Some singer from Blackpool. Yet Andrew and his family never made me feel like I didn't belong. They are the loveliest people you could meet. As you might have anticipated, I completely fell in love with their dog.

After rehearsing our songs and dance routines at the BBC TV Centre earlier in the week, we performed live for the Lord and his esteemed audience. We sang 'Oom-Pah-Pah' and 'Things Ain't What They Used To Be' in groups, and we also performed an acting piece to prove just how Nancy-like we could be. It was scary stuff: singing on stage in front of this highly critical crowd, who were scrutinizing every move we made and every note we sang.

I have to say, though, in spite of the pressure, the buzz during the night was electric. The show went superbly and the performers all got on really well; there wasn't a hint of catty competitiveness.

Once the showcase was over, there was nothing else we could do. It was down to Lord Lloyd-Webber and his panel of judges to decide which of the eighteen would be whittled down to the final twelve.

That evening, I had a sleepless night at the local Hilton Hotel, where we were all staying, as I wondered what choices would be made. I couldn't help myself, but lay there imagining what it might be like to star in the West End. It felt so close this time; I could almost smell the theatre. I was hungry for it, and really didn't want to be one of the six who would miss out.

The next day was judgement day. Lord Lloyd-Webber, John Barrowman, Denise Van Outen, producer Cameron Mackintosh and new panellist Barry Humphries (Dame Edna Everage's alter ego, who has twice played Fagin in the West End) gathered to debate which girls they thought were strong enough to compete in the studio shows.

Meanwhile, we were all waiting anxiously in another room. I tried to keep everyone buoyant with a few bubbly quips, but we were painfully aware that this might be the end of our journey. I looked around me and I could see that there were some very talented contenders. This wasn't the time to fret about the competition, though: I had to be confident and believe in myself. And I did. I really thought I had what it took, at least to get into the final stages.

Graham Norton came to join us and told us that the Lord and his panel needed to hear some of us again. That made us all feel a little edgy. Maybe the choice was proving harder than we thought. Were the girls they wanted to hear from again weak, or were they favourites?

Among the contestants called back for a second audition was a Northern Irish girl called Jessie Buckley. I'd rated her from the beginning. She was pretty and she had a great voice. If there was a question over her ability, where did that leave the rest of us?

It turned out that the panel were concerned that, at eighteen, Jessie might not have the maturity for the role. When she sang for him again, Andrew told her that she had blown him away.

Eventually, we were told that the judges had made their final decision. In a matter of minutes, we were going to find out which of us were going through to the studio shows.

One by one, we were called in to meet Andrew Lloyd Webber. Jessie made it through, and was over the moon. I wasn't surprised by any of the girls who came out smiling, as they were all strong vocalists and had fire in their bellies.

Then it was my turn. Standing in front of one of the biggest stars in theatre, I was in awe. I didn't know what to think. Would I have to go back to my normal life tomorrow – or would I continue on my journey?

'Are you ever sad?' Andrew asked me. 'It's important that this bubbly person doesn't get in the way of Nancy.'

My heart sank. Was this Andrew's way of saying I wasn't right for the role? Immediately, I started having verbal diarrhoea – going on about how if anyone hurt an animal, that would upset me, and how I can never watch a film that features an animal that gets hurt. You know when you're speaking, and even if the voice in your head says 'Stop!' you carry on? Well, that was me. I wanted to explain to Andrew that there were more sides to Jodie; that during my life I *had* experienced tears and heartache; and that the happy Jodie I showed to the world was just one aspect of me.

Luckily, I didn't need to bother, because he next said the words: 'Jodie, you could be Nancy.'

Result! I had done it. I couldn't believe it. This was the best news I had heard in a long time. I really wanted to scoop Andrew up in my arms and spin him around, but then I thought better of it as it's not really the kind of thing you do to a musical legend.

The first thing I did was telephone my family. I still didn't truly believe I'd got through, even though it turned out that the BBC had sent a film crew to watch my parents receive the call. Ecstatic is not the word for their reaction: I could hear my mum and dad crying with joy, and they had gathered quite a few of my friends at the house too, so they were a noisy bunch all together. I was so pleased that I had made them proud.

The question was: how long would it last? How long would I survive in the competition ... now that it was down to a public vote?

23
Show Time

After all the excitement of making it to the live finals, there was something of an anti-climax, as we had to keep everything a secret. A couple of weeks later, however, the twelve finalists were moved into the 'Nancy' house in London, which was located on the riverbank in Hammersmith, and the show began in earnest.

Our new home was a seven-bedroom property, owned by a guy who still lived there, but in another part of the house. We never saw much of him to be honest.

Most of the other girls were really nice, and we all seemed to bond pretty well with one another. Although we were battling it out to win *I'd Do Anything*, we never got so competitive that we put laxative in each other's tea, or anything like that. All the girls – perhaps bar one – were lovely and genuine and supportive. Just one proved to be a bit of a prima donna, who irritated us by being moody in the house, but then became all sweetness and light once the cameras were on. If there's one thing I can't abide, it's people who are two-faced – but I think those people always get found out in the end anyway. With me, what you see is what you get. I'm not going to pull the wool over anyone's eyes.

I shared a room with Fran, and we had a ball. Amazingly, we even had our own walk-in wardrobe: how Carrie Bradshaw! The contestant with whom I really hit it off, though, was

Ashley Russell. I love that girl. We really connected and are still very close to this day.

Ash and I would laugh all the time. It was infectious. We'd giggle at all sorts, and our relationship kept us grounded and relaxed. As we had a film crew joining us every day, we had to do silly stuff, such as making sock puppets. Why? I have no idea, but it seemed like a good plan at the time, and it certainly helped to take our minds off the fear of the upcoming series.

Generally, all the girls had an enjoyable time, which was a relief. When you put a group of lasses together, anything can happen – cat fights at dawn, you name it – but we all got on. When the camera crews weren't there, we'd prepare food together in the kitchen, slump on the couch and watch the telly, or slink away to our rooms and practise singing.

We didn't have much time to settle into the new house because we had to go straight into rehearsals, and do several photo shoots for the pre-publicity of the show. While it was work, I actually enjoyed the PR aspect of the programme. I really relished taking part in the photo shoots and the interviews – us girlies had such a good laugh. If there's one thing I like to do, it's talk; and so whenever I met a journalist, I gave them exactly what they wanted.

Then came the moment when we were shown our Nancy costumes for the first time. I was so excited. The dress was beautiful, and really put me in a Nancy mindset. I was especially pleased to discover that my frock was purple, a colour that has been constant in my life. I had a violet school uniform at Elmslie, and my costumes for both *Spooktacular* and Disney's *Hercules* were the same shade. I hoped that was a good omen.

As the first show approached, the producers told us what to expect from the next ten weeks. Our schedule would involve intense training all week long, as we rehearsed for the live broadcast; then on a Wednesday or Thursday, we'd have to do a 'challenge', which would be filmed. Come Saturday, we'd be at the BBC studios all day. If you thought we had time off on the Sunday, you'd be wrong. We went straight back to work and would start on the new batch of songs for the following week's performances.

The days leading up to the first show, scheduled for 29 March 2008, were like a roller coaster. As we neared the big day, it felt like we were reaching a peak, like we were cresting a summit before shooting off on an incredible journey. I couldn't wait for it to begin.

That Saturday morning, I was up bright and early. A car came to pick us up, and took us to BBC TV Centre, where we were met by a guy called Michael Canning, who would be our contact for the day, talking us through the things we needed to do and making sure we were all right.

The initial item on the itinerary was a session in the studio, for our very first rehearsal in the space in which we would actually perform. During this, we had to wear these coloured bibs that matched our Nancy colour, so the crew could tell who was who. After that, we headed into make-up, where a girl called Kate – who, bizarrely enough, shared the same birthday as me – transformed me into someone presentable enough to be seen on TV.

All dolled up and looking like a bunch of wannabe Nancys, we then had another rehearsal – this time, in our dresses. The final stage after that was for us to have our hair and make-up touched up for the live show, which was, by now, excruciatingly close.

Moments before going live, we were all like giggly school-girls backstage. We'd been rehearsing day and night for the past two weeks and were exhausted, but the buzz in the studio really pepped us up.

As well as searching for an actress to play Nancy, Andrew Lloyd Webber and Cameron Mackintosh were simultaneously casting three boys in the role of Oliver, though the young lads in the running would not be subjected to a public vote. The twelve 'Olivers' now joined us to open the show with a rousing rendition of 'I'd Do Anything' – and then each of the Nancys performed a solo song.

I was second up with Adele's 'Chasing Pavements'. Although I had butterflies in my stomach and my hands were sweating around the microphone, I was happy with my performance and felt I had given it my best shot. Vocally, I thought I'd been strong and I definitely felt like I'd been telling a story.

When the song ended, the audience went wild – and I knew for a fact that I had done well. I looked at my family and Steve in the crowd and they were on their feet. They were smiling so broadly that I knew my performance had come across as I'd hoped. But the audience in the studio were only part of the show. It was Andrew and his panel that I needed to impress, not to mention the viewers at home, who would have to pick up their phones to vote to keep their favourites in the series. Without their support, my dream would be over before it began.

Reassuringly, the panel seemed to like me. John Barrowman said, 'I love you to death, you connected with everyone and told the story – that's Nancy.' Denise Van Outen commented, 'Nancy needs to have a lot of life experience and I see that coming through in your performance. It was brilliant.' Barry Humphries, meanwhile, added: 'You've got that toughness and also a tenderness. A beautiful performance.'

All good stuff – but I wanted to hear what Andrew had thought. After all, he was the man who had the final say in the dreaded sing-off. When he remarked that I could definitely play Nancy, I was thrilled. Walking offstage, I felt like I was floating on air.

As I watched the rest of the show from backstage, though, I started to wonder if I had done enough to stay on another week. Would the TV audience have taken to me? I could only hope they had.

After the credits rolled, we had to run through the results show, which was a good thing as it helped to keep my mind off thinking that it could be me going home ... until we came to rehearsing 'the moment of truth', that is. In order to practise the evictee's finale, the producers had to select a contestant to pretend to go out. They chose a different girl each week, but on that first Saturday, I was the one in the spotlight. It made me feel sick. Then, from the studio audience, who were still in their seats, a voice called out: 'That will never f**king happen.'

The voice belonged to a guy called Ian Temple, whom I've since nicknamed Shirley. To hear someone give me so much support instilled in me the confidence to carry on. I can never thank him enough. I don't know exactly what it was about his encouraging cry, but that was the moment when I really started to believe that I could see this through to the end.

In the real results show later that evening, the Nancys all stood on stage, just as we'd rehearsed, waiting to find out who would be in the bottom two. The suspense was painful. As Graham started to announce the names of the lucky girls who were to survive another week, I stared blankly ahead of me. I didn't want to catch anyone's eye: neither that of the other girls, nor of friends and family in the audience. If I had, I think I would have burst into tears on the spot.

When Graham called my name, I was shocked. I knew I had performed well for the studio audience, but the viewing public made the final decision. Who knew what they were seeing on their TV screens at home? It was such a different medium to live theatre.

Amy and Francesca, my room-mate, were the two girls who received the lowest phone votes. To fight for survival, the pair of them had to sing one last song for Lord Lloyd-Webber. As they tried to outdo each other on 'Tell Me On A Sunday', the rest of us sat on the sidelines, all holding hands, not really wanting to see one of our gang leave. Of course, we knew that was the whole point of the programme, but it's never nice to see someone's dreams come to a sudden and very public end. What was even more terrifying was that we realized that, at some point, we'd all be in this position: fighting for our lives to stay on the show.

In the end, Andrew chose to eliminate Amy. She was distraught, and her tears made us appreciate just how important this chance was to all of us. This was an opportunity that only a handful of girls had been offered, but there was still only one role up for grabs. Every week, there was a danger that our own dream could be snatched away. I knew there and then that I had to fight my hardest to stay in the series. From that moment, I became very focused and made sure I rehearsed as much as was physically possible.

As the weeks rolled past, the competition got tougher. The hardest part was saying goodbye to the Nancys. The worst week for me was week seven, when my pal Ashley was eliminated. I couldn't believe that she was going. I'd thought she was excellent and had a real chance, but I guess she wasn't what Andrew and Cameron were looking for.

I remember going back to the house that night and just hugging Ashley. We were both sobbing because we knew that she was no longer on the same journey. It sounds dramatic, I know, but you have to remember that we were in a kind of bubble, so everything affected us more than it normally would have done. I was convinced that I would see Ashley again once the series was over, because I knew I had made a good friend in her, but at that moment, it felt like the end of the world.

My favourite week was when Rachel, Ashley and I strutted our stuff to 'Man, I Feel Like A Woman'. The girls were the best fun when we all worked together. Although we were battling for the one role, as I've said before, there really wasn't a sense of competitiveness. Sure, we wanted to win, but we were never devious or bitchy. We never snapped the heel off another contestant's shoe or hovered behind them at the top of that staircase, hands held aloft!

For the Shania Twain performance, we had to use these canes in the choreography. We kept dropping them during rehearsals – I think Kevan despaired – but it was such a good laugh. Come the show, we managed to keep the canes in our hands. Mischievously, we changed the lyrics a little bit, singing 'Come on, Andrew' to the Lord himself as we descended the steps. That was the same night I almost fell down the stairs when my toe got twisted. Luckily, I managed to stay upright.

To enable the audience to judge our capability to play Nancy, not only did we sing songs on the live programmes, but we also went on weekly missions, in which we took on a series of challenges that required various skills. One week, we had to face our fears by acting with rats; another time, we had to perform a love scene from the stage musical *Hairspray* with its star, former Joseph wannabe Ben James Ellis.

Embarrassingly, this mission was done in front of our fathers, which I found particularly cringeworthy. There's nothing worse than having to get intimate with some guy in front of your dad, even if you are just acting. It's every girl's worst nightmare.

Nevertheless, I understood why we were asked to do it. If we had to perform a sexually charged scene in front of thousands of people, the producers had to ensure that we wouldn't clam up and get all self-conscious. If we could do what was needed in front of our dads without feeling or looking uncomfortable, then we'd definitely be able to cope with thousands of eyes watching our every move.

In other weeks, our fitness was tested in a rowing task, which took me straight back to my days on *The Biggest Loser*; and on another occasion our comedy muscles were flexed in a masterclass with Phill Jupitus.

The latter was a great task for me because I had to get up

on stage and try to make people laugh – something that was all too familiar from my time doing cabaret. Fortunately, all my previous work on the club circuit had truly given me the gift of the gab, and I did well. Phill told me afterwards that he thought I was pretty funny, which was such an honour. I felt so comfortable being up on stage and improvising. That's what I love. I may not have been to stage school, but my time in the clubs has given me training of a different sort.

My favourite mission of all, though, was when we had to convince Barbara Windsor that we could pull off a cockney accent by performing a scene from the musical *Blood Brothers* in a London pub. I got to meet 'Babs' properly, and she was such a lovely woman, who really supported us and gave us a lot of sound advice. She was just as you expected her to be: tiny and bubbly and full of beans. I was pleased that she was exactly like the Barbara Windsor I'd come to love in those *Carry On* films; I think I would have been very disappointed if she had been arrogant.

The series wasn't all work, work, work. Sometimes, the BBC would take us off for a treat. On 12 May, we went to the premiere of the film of *Sex and the City*. I couldn't believe that I was rubbing shoulders with the stars of one of my favourite TV shows. Sarah Jessica Parker looked so stylish, just like she is in the programme. I was speechless to be breathing the same air as her.

Yet even that extraordinary experience paled in comparison to the night I met the most gorgeous man in the world – George Clooney. Yep, you read that right: George Clooney. One week, we were invited to the premiere of his film *Leatherheads*, and we got to meet him and shake his hand. He was so charismatic; I instantly fell in love. There I was, flashing my gnashers at the planet's sexiest man – I had to pinch myself to make sure it was really happening.

Sadly, our meeting was very brief, but that moment will remain a cherished memory until my dying day. I still haven't washed my hand and sometimes I like to smell my fingers and remember ... nah, not really.

Sitting in the cinema, both times, I was totally star-struck by these amazing legends from Hollywood. I had come a long way. I would never have imagined in a million years that one day I would be invited to film premieres. This was what dreams were made of.

Over the course of the series of *I'd Do Anything*, as you probably know, we all had to sing a variety of numbers, from musicals and films, and from the charts, past and present. My favourite performance was when I sang the Stephen Sondheim classic 'Send in the Clowns', from his musical *A Little Night Music*, in week three.

It could have been my downfall; the biggest mistake of the lot of them. The performance showed such a different side to me than the audience had seen up to that point. Would they accept it? I knew people thought that I only had a bubbly personality – this was my chance to prove to them that there was much more to me than that. So I adored performing that song, and I always say it was the turnaround in the series for me.

The panel, for a start, loved it. I was always conscious that Andrew had worried about me being 'the funny girl' – he'd expressed that even before we got to the live shows – so I was determined to demonstrate that there was more to me than cracking jokes and being camp. And it worked. I was so pleased that I had finally shown everyone that I wasn't a one-trick pony, who could only slap my thigh and give a cheeky wink.

That particular show was also a memorable one for me because, after the cameras had stopped rolling, Steve decided to get down on one knee and propose. It came as a shock, because I genuinely wasn't expecting it, even though a Sunday tabloid had run a silly story claiming he had asked BBC bosses if he could propose on screen.

When he whisked me out to the toilet corridor at the BBC – ah, the romance! – with a pink piece of paper, I just wondered what he was doing. He had talked about our getting engaged previously, but I had asked him to leave it until after the series was over: I can't tell you the amount of pressure you are under as a contestant, and I didn't want that to spoil anything.

Nevertheless, things had been going well with him for a while by that time, and I had really fallen for him. He'd been there for me every week and was really behind me: not bad for a guy I'd known for only a few months. He was close to my family, and would travel down with them every week to watch the show. To me, that meant a lot. He had integrated so well with Mum, Dad and Marko that I was already beginning to think of him as part of the family. It just felt right. So when I read the sheet of pink paper that he handed me, on which was written a poem that concluded with a proposal, I said, 'Yes, I will marry you.'

Now, I know what you're thinking. Had I not learned any lessons from my doomed experience with Darren? Clearly not. But this time, everything appeared to be perfect. I loved Steve and he seemed like such a sorted gentleman. What could go wrong?

I ran off to tell my mum, and she was thrilled for me. Yet it hadn't been a surprise to her: Steve had gone round to see my dad to ask him for my hand in marriage. My parents liked that a lot. They thought it was very chivalrous and romantic. So, they were genuinely pleased that I had said 'yes', especially when they saw how happy I was.

Steve's mum was at the studio that night. He had flown her all the way from Spain, so I should have known something fishy was going on. She was a lovely woman and seemed to take a shine to me.

It looked like things were really going well. My career was on the up and now, finally, my love life was headed in the right direction too.

When I told the rest of the girls about Steve's proposal, they were overjoyed for me, and burst into an impromptu performance of 'I'm Getting Married in the Morning'. Theatre types, eh?

24

The Winner Takes It All

After nine incredible weeks, the *I'd Do Anything* journey was about to come to an end. One of three girls would soon be told that she had won the role of a lifetime, and would play Nancy in the West End.

After all the eliminations, just Jessie Buckley, the Northern Irish girl, Sam Barks – a seventeen-year-old from the Isle of Man – and I were left. It was hard to believe that I had made it through to the final, but something inside me told me I deserved it. I had been consistently good on every show, and the judges had always liked me. Also, I had never been in a sing-off, so I knew that the public had taken to me, which was a real endorsement.

With just a few hours to go before we found out the final result, I was buzzing with anticipation. I so wanted to win; I didn't want to let this opportunity slip through my fingers. I had come too close to lose it now, and would be devastated to miss out at such a late stage. The three of us had told each other that we were all winners to get so far, but in my head, the only real winner was the one who was going to be Nancy. I desperately hoped that winner would be me.

Yet my confidence had been knocked, despite my faith in my voice and acting skills. The day before the final, Andrew Lloyd Webber had revealed to the *Mirror* newspaper that Cameron Mackintosh was concerned about my curvaceous figure.

Andrew had revealed, 'Cameron thinks she is a bit too big and has more or less said so.'

When I read that, I was absolutely mortified. For years, I had battled with my weight and struggled to be taken seriously. Even though I had now lost almost half my body weight from when I was at my heaviest, I was still being criticized. I was gutted that my size remained an issue. I knew I wasn't as thin as I had been when I'd come out of the *Biggest Loser* house, but I was nowhere near the 22 stone I'd once been. Besides, who was to say that Nancy had to be a pipe cleaner? I'm a size fourteen: an average woman.

The comments really hurt me, and I was worried that Cameron's opinion could mean that I was out of the running. After all, he was the producer and, ultimately, had the final say. The public might vote me through, but that didn't mean Cameron would be happy about it.

On the plus side, Andrew defended me in the same article, saying he thought I had both the vocal talent and character for the role. 'Jodie could be anybody's idea of Nancy – I can see it absolutely,' he said. 'She has got a lovely voice and a super personality. She has experience as well.'

That blip aside, the days leading up to the final had been truly awe-inspiring. Mid week, Sam, Jessie and I had been whisked off to Paris for one-to-one tutorials with the musical legend Liza Minnelli. I have loved 'Liza with a Z' all of my life – figures, doesn't it? – and to meet her in the flesh and have her listen to us sing was an incredible experience. Better still, to hear her say she liked our voices ...

I was last to have my tutorial with her. She seemed so happy to see me and gave me a big hug. Then she asked me to sing her classic song 'Maybe This Time'. It was weird, when she was standing right there in front of me, to perform a song that's so closely associated with her. Yet she seemed to like what I was doing and gently rocked to the music as I sang.

Afterwards, she gave me a little advice about making some

of the phrasing softer. As I left, she said to me, 'If you ever play anywhere, I will come and see you.' To hear those words come out of the mouth of a singing superstar like Liza, whom I had looked up to for so many years, was amazing. I will never forget that moment for the rest of my days. I've no idea if she's coming to see *Oliver!*, but let me say right here, she can be my guest any time.

Back in London, once the final programme began – at 6 p.m. on 31 May 2008 – I didn't have time to be nervous. I raced through the opening numbers. The three boys chosen for the role of Oliver had been announced the week before, and each of them performed a duet with a Nancy finalist that night. I relished my song with Laurence Jeffcoate: 'Getting To Know You' from *The King And I*. I also sang my heart out when Sam, Jessie and I performed 'Maybe This Time' – hoping that Liza Minnelli, if she was watching somewhere, would be proud of me.

For my crucial solo spot, I sang Dusty Springfield's 'Son of a Preacher Man': one of Andrew Lloyd Webber's favourite songs. With this, I finally managed to persuade Cameron that I was a contender.

'Jodie has convinced me that she could make a Nancy,' Cameron announced, filling me with joy. 'You absolutely deserve to be in the final.'

Andrew, meanwhile, added: 'It was a very, very, very good performance. You have an outsize talent, and a very strong voice.' I was elated – until he tacked on to the end: 'I don't know if it's going to be enough tonight, but it might be.'

Well, at least they recognized that I was worthy of a place in the final. That was something. At that stage, I couldn't fret about it further because there was nothing more I could do. The phone lines were open, and it was now up to the viewers to choose which two contestants would make it through to the second show later that same evening.

We didn't have to wait long to find out the result. At the

end of the first show, Graham Norton revealed which of the three of us was going no further. I closed my eyes, praying my hardest that I was still in with a chance. When Graham called Sam's name, I had mixed emotions. I was jubilant, of course, that I was in the final, but I was also distraught that Sam had missed out.

Yet I quickly pulled myself together – I had to. This was a competition and there was still a goal to be reached. I wanted to be Nancy and I couldn't rest on my laurels. This was make-or-break time.

In the second show, Jessie and I both sang Nancy's powerful ballad from *Oliver!*, 'As Long As He Needs Me'. I thought I pulled off a good performance.

Incidentally, how I sang it then is totally different to how I sing it now in the stage production. When you live the role of Nancy in the story of *Oliver!* and experience what she goes through, the words and sentiment really do mean so much more. It's not a song to win a reality show – it's a song about an unhappy woman who is controlled by a man; the kind of woman of whom you ask, 'Why are you still with him?' and she replies, 'Because I love him.' It's tragic.

We also performed our final solo numbers. Mine was Whitney's 'I Have Nothing'. I must say, I would never have chosen that number myself, but it turned out to be the perfect selection.

The way the song choices usually worked on the show was that we contestants would draw up a list of songs we wanted to sing, and then the producers would have a big production meeting at which all the songs would be decided and allocated. What was remarkable was that the team knew our voices better than we did, and of course they knew what made for a show-stopping number, so they'd often suggest songs to us too.

When they told me I was down to sing Whitney at the final, I was petrified. I mean, come on, she is *the* diva. Could

I rise to the challenge, or would I just embarrass myself? The team gave me loads of encouragement, and in the end I'd like to think I pulled it off rather gallantly. I really couldn't get over how supportive the BBC crew was; throughout the series, they treated us like true royalty. I could never have pulled it out the bag without their backing.

Once we'd sung our last notes, that was it. We could do no more. The decision was now out of our hands. The nation would decide whether it was Jessie or me who would land that spectacular West End role.

Before the winner was announced, as Jessie and I stood nervously on the central staircase for the very last time, Graham asked the panel whom they had personally chosen as their Nancy. I was thrilled when John and Denise picked me, but disappointed when Barry, Cameron *and* Andrew opted for Jessie. Did that mean they would be unhappy if I was the winner?

I didn't have time to dwell on that for long – because Graham revealed that he had the result. My breath was short by now. I was exhilarated. My mouth was dry and my mind was whizzing. In fact, I felt like I was drunk, but I hadn't had a sip all night.

'The winning Nancy is …' Graham began.

I glanced over at my mum, who was looking so excited. I hoped I wasn't about to disappoint her.

'… Jodie.'

Oh my God! I could not believe what I had just heard. He had read out my name. The shock was such that I almost collapsed. I had done it. I had won the show: beaten 10,000 girls to land the role of Nancy. I was going to star in London's prestigious West End; work with legends from the musical world … all my dreams had come true. This was surreal. I could not take it in. I was suddenly a lass from Blackpool who had made good.

I screamed in the most primal way – and you know what?

I could feel a bit of pee come out at the same time. I was so overwhelmed, you can't blame me for it. Embarrassingly, midway through relating the story the following week on *The Graham Norton Show*, I realized I was sat next to Hollywood superstar Susan Sarandon. I died a little inside at that moment. Where was my decorum?

The final cherry on top of my win was that it seemed I had convinced Andrew and Cameron to believe in me at last. Graham went to Andrew for a comment on the result and he enthused: 'Jodie was always going to be the people's choice. I think people love her; they love her open personality. I think they relate to that and I think that's what makes her Nancy for the public. That and her very, very strong voice.'

Cameron – my new boss, unbelievably – said, 'I'm thrilled for Jodie. She is obviously the public's view of what they want to see as Nancy. She'll give a terrific performance and I really look forward to putting her into training and getting her into rehearsals.'

Those were the words I had been waiting for. While I wasn't 100 per cent sure that I had immediately convinced Andrew and Cameron that I was the best woman for the job, at least I now had the opportunity to prove it to them. Now I felt like a true winner. I had landed my dream job – and I was engaged to be married, too. Everything was going so well. I felt so lucky that I thought I probably ought to choose some lottery numbers, just in case!

After the show – which I closed with another performance of 'As Long As He Needs Me', in damp pants, as the ticker tape rained down – I attended a press conference, during which I smiled at journos like an air hostess. Then the entire cast and crew of *I'd Do Anything* came together for a wrap party (not a 'rat party', as I'd first thought) and I enjoyed a few glasses of champers to celebrate the news.

It was a truly great night. The BBC bar had been decorated with balloons and set up like Fagin's den. It was fabulous ... and sad at the same time, because I felt like I was saying goodbye to a big family that I had been a part of for so many months. I was going to miss everyone: the producers, the hair and make-up people, the cameramen; everyone who had worked so hard to make us look good and feel safe and comfortable. I didn't want to say goodbye – I liked it there in the Nancy bubble.

At the party, Denise and John both congratulated me, and confided that I had always been one of their favourite Nancys, which made me feel very special. I have to say, Denise is so grounded. Throughout the competition, she was always there to offer advice. Both she and Graham Norton are really wonderful people. I love Graham to bits (and his dogs, Bailey and Madge). During *I'd Do Anything*, I really hit it off with Graham's mate, Carl, too. Oh, we got on like a house on fire. Bless him, he even wore a 'Jodie' T-shirt to the final. That meant so much to me.

I didn't see Barry Humphries at the bash. In all honesty, I wasn't that bothered by his apparent absence, as I never took to him personally. I adored all the other judges, but I often wondered why Barry was there.

Cameron and Andrew, however, took the opportunity at the do to tell me that they were pleased with the public's choice and that they had high hopes for me when I finally stepped out on stage. While their comments boosted my confidence, I was still determined to prove to Cameron that I could be the best Nancy he could have hoped for. I may not have been as thin as Jessie, but I could certainly give the role some guts and real emotion. He had lit a fire in my belly, and I resolved to show him that I was exactly what he'd been looking for.

After the party, Sam decided to stay with her family, while Jessie and I went back to the Nancy house and viewed the final on tape. It was weird watching it back, as it didn't seem like I was watching myself. It was a bit like an out-of-body experience. Seeing Graham break the news was amazing to watch on screen – I really did look surprised. My eyes were wide and my gob was almost on the floor. Not a very flattering look, I will admit, but a genuine one.

When I woke up the next morning, it still hadn't sunk in that I had won the show. Tears of happiness flowed when I remembered the events of the night before – and when I met up with my family and Steve, I couldn't contain my emotions. This was the most incredible thing that had ever happened to me. I simply didn't know how to deal with it.

Very quickly, however, the BBC helped me to come to terms with it. My first task was to find an agent, who would represent me in my new career and guide me through the uncharted waters that lay ahead. The BBC team was very supportive in this minefield of a challenge, and arranged for me to meet lots of great people.

In the end, I decided to sign up with Gavin Barker, of Gavin Barker Associates (GBA). I had got to know Gav over the course of the series, as he also represents John Barrowman and, consequently, was often at the *I'd Do Anything* studio on a Saturday night. I had a gut instinct that he was the right man for the job.

My mum was elated by my choice when I told her. As my triumph meant that I would eventually have to move to London, she had already started fretting about how I would cope. But with Gavin behind me, she felt confident that I'd be fine. Indeed, when Gavin next saw her, he gave her the warm reassurance that I was 'part of the GBA family now', and that put her mind at rest. And it's true: the whole team really is like a big family, with Steven and Michelle at the office being just as welcoming and friendly as Mr Barker himself. They're real pals.

So there I was: the future star of the West End and the future Mrs Steve Greengrass. Could life get any better?

As it would turn out: no. The Curse of Jodie Prenger was about to strike again.

25

I'm Gonna Wash That Man Right Out of My Hair

Let's talk about Steve. When he proposed to me during *I'd Do Anything*, I was over a million moons. I really, really thought I had found a good man this time. After twenty-eight years and all the dodgy blokes I'd dated, I thought I'd finally been able to work out who was right for me. But clearly my radar is still not up to scratch.

Let me take you back to when I first met him. My friend Alison and I were having a girlie night in one evening when we saw an advert on Facebook for a dating website that was popular with men who were successful and wealthy. I decided to sign up.

Now, don't get me wrong. I wasn't on the prowl for some craggy old codger with a fat bank balance and a heart condition. I was just looking for someone who was successful and sorted. I always say that a man who has made his own money is a fella who has got a good head on his shoulders. That's an attractive quality. The bulge of his wallet is never as important. Whether someone was to give me a Bentley or a key ring that said 'I Love You, Jodie' on it, I'd hold on to that key ring for ever. I'm sentimental like that.

I'd had enough of meeting chaps who were messed up. I wanted to find a man who had a good career and a positive outlook on life. I wanted a man to love me and to give me kids. I'd seen my mum and dad graft hard all their lives to be able to afford the wonderful childhood they gave my brother and me. Like them, I wanted, one day, to be able to provide for my kids in the best way I possibly could – which meant that I didn't want to get lumped with a man whom I had to support as well.

Looking through the site, Alison and I came across several nice guys. Some were young and dashing. Before I met Steve, I rendezvoused with a guy from the site who was lovely. Nothing happened between us, but we stayed in touch and he is now one of my best friends in London, who is always there for me whenever I'm in trouble or I need some advice. You see, not everyone on the Internet is dodgy. Some can be decent, genuine guys. You just have to seek them out.

Steve and I enjoyed a bit of email banter at first, and then decided to meet for a bite to eat in Manchester. He was quite a sweet man, though certainly not as cute as he was in his profile picture. But hey, I probably didn't look quite the same as in my pic, either. Who does? As we chatted, I decided that he seemed like a good guy.

At the end of the night, we went back to his hotel and had a quick snog. Having done a round of shots on Deansgate Locks before we'd made our way back, though, I passed out almost as soon as we got there, which I can't say was the most endearing thing to do. In the morning, all I wanted was to head for the bathroom. I can't drink like I used to, full stop.

I definitely wanted to see Steve again. We went on to enjoy a series of dates that of course coincided with the run of *I'd Do Anything*, and he proposed after we'd known each other for just nine weeks.

When he popped the question, I was swept away. He really seemed to love me; he told me all the time. I was living in this wonderful Nancy world – and I was naive. Looking back, we hadn't even lived together, so what the hell was I thinking in accepting?

After my win, I should have been on cloud nine, but it turned out that my friends had been keeping some suspicions about Steve quiet so that I could concentrate on the show. Now that it was over, I began to find out things that I just didn't want to believe. Conflicting stories were emerging and it was these that ultimately ended our relationship. There were too many things that didn't add up.

At the exact same time, I had loads of media interviews to do to publicize my triumph on *I'd Do Anything*. As I went from studio to studio and talked nineteen to the dozen about my excitement in winning, I had all this other stuff going round in my head. I couldn't talk directly to Steve about it as my schedule was so crazy, but we exchanged a series of increasingly fraught text messages.

It was then that I cut him out of my life. I didn't dump him via text as he subsequently suggested. I just stopped returning his calls. A bit of a drippy way to do it, admittedly, but he was beginning to scare me.

When he could get no response from me, he started sending intimidating texts, threatening to sell an interview about me to *The Sun*. The threats became so constant that the police were forced to intervene.

Once we had split, he got in touch with a company called Cash 4 Your Story, who can get you in the papers, and he sold his story, claiming I would do anything to be famous and suggesting that I had used our relationship to win votes on the programme. All this came out of the blue for me.

I think the problem with Steve was that he got caught up in the whole fame thing. I was never that fussed about it. But I suspect he loved the attention.

All I want to say is, people don't know what went on with him. I don't want to waste too much time thinking about him.

He is my past now: just another guy who took advantage of me.

Why are men so difficult? I am lucky and blessed in my career, I know that, but when it comes to fellas – oh, I have had some terrible chaps.

I guess all this stands me in good stead for the role of Nancy. That's the only bright side I can see. Yet while it might be great practice for the part, I'm sick of having to deal with it. From now on, I am getting my mum and Angie to vet any potential boyfriends before I date them.

I will keep looking for Mr Right, though. I guess he is out there somewhere ... that Mills and Boon-style romance hasn't died in me yet.

26

London Life

With men relegated to the back of my mind, I decided to focus on what was important – getting down to work.

Rehearsals for *Oliver!* weren't due to start until late October, so I had a lot of time before I was due to slip on my red Nancy dress. Amazingly, I found my work schedule fast filling up with exciting theatrical opportunities. Friends said to me at the time, 'Surely you need a holiday after all that has happened to you?' But I always responded, 'Working and mixing in these circles is better than any holiday I could imagine, as I'm finally getting to do everything I have always wanted to.'

First up was Andrew Lloyd Webber's new baby, *Phantom of the Opera 2*. Now, I'm not entirely sure if that is what the show is going to be called in the end. Basically, it's his follow-up to *Phantom*, so I'll call it that for now – sorry, Lord Lloyd-Webber, if I've made it sound like a *Jaws* sequel.

I was so thrilled to work with Andrew on this wonderful project. It was different to *I'd Do Anything* because this was a real job: I was actually collaborating with one of the most famous men in the land of musicals. Who'd have thought it? Me, Jodie Prenger, living and breathing in the same world as a lord. Fancy!

Fortunately, I wasn't alone. Also part of the cast were

Rachel, Niamh, Ashley, Jessie and Sam from *I'd Do Anything* – so I wasn't the only one walking around with my gob hitting the floor every two seconds.

Although we'd at first thought there might be a possibility that we were being groomed to appear in the eagerly anticipated new musical, it turned out that our services had been called upon to help Andrew fine-tune the score. We'd sing through the songs for him to see if the music worked. More often than not, it did.

Well, what did you expect? It's Andrew Lloyd Webber. Everything he touches turns to gold. I swear, the minute you hear the songs, you will be singing them for days if not weeks afterwards.

Once we'd rehearsed the music, we all headed to Andrew's mansion in Sydmonton, where we put on a mini version of the production – in the very theatre in which we'd staged the crucial *I'd Do Anything* showcase, our performances in which had secured us our places in the live shows. It brought back lots of happy memories.

We were under the direction of a rather fabulously camp guy called Jack O'Brien, who had previously directed the Broadway production of *Hairspray*. Now, I'm not exaggerating when I say Jack was camp. With his brash, broad, New York twang and flamboyant swagger, all he was missing was a feather boa wrapped around his neck. Of course, I adore camp so I just fell in love with him straight away. What can I say? I must have been a drag queen in a previous life.

We all had a great time at Sydmonton. That's partly because Andrew and his wife Madeleine are the perfect hosts. The pair of them are completely grounded – and their children are so well-mannered, you wouldn't believe it. Andrew is a real family man, and clearly so very close to his wife. God, I'm beginning to sound like my nan when I say things like 'well-mannered', but they really are a lovely, friendly family.

After two weeks' rehearsal, we finally performed *Phantom 2* before an audience of specially invited guests, who included famous folks like Angus Deayton, Arlene Phillips from *Strictly Come Dancing*, Ben Elton, Sir Tim Rice and Janet Street-Porter, to name just a few. The experience was joyous. The songs went down a storm, as I'd expected, and although there were no more than forty or so people in the audience, I thoroughly enjoyed belting out the fantastic tunes for them. If I hadn't wanted to work in musical theatre before, that night most certainly clinched it for me.

Something I had to squeeze into my packed schedule was a rather major house move. Blackpool is a fantastic place to live, but it certainly isn't within commuting distance of the West End. Moving to London was brilliant, but also very strange for me. Don't forget that I was leaving a household that contained a chatty mother and father, squawking parrots, barking dogs … and coming down south to live on my own.

When I first moved into the apartment off Tottenham Court Road that Cameron had offered me (I later moved into a place of my own), the change of environment was marked. I missed the noise and bustle of home; I missed the company. The silence of the house really got to me, so I would leave the telly on almost all the time, just so there was a bit of noise in the background. Of course, my family kept telling me they were only a phone call away, and I certainly made the most of my free time by calling Mum, Dad and Marko. My telephone bill was huge.

Occasionally, I'd have the rest of the Nancys round to see what they were up to. Since the series, most of them have found work in show business, so in some ways, we were all winners after all. Rachel landed a role in *We Will Rock You*; Amy is starring in the new *Sister Act* musical; Tara toured *Joseph and the Amazing Technicolor Dreamcoat*; Sam toured *Cabaret*; Jessie appeared in *A Little Night Music*; Fran is in *Can't Smile Without You*; Cleo got a part in *Dirty Dancing*; Keisha went to train at Mountview Academy of Theatre Arts; Sarah is in the ensemble of *Oliver!*, and the Nancy understudy; Niamh played Snow White in panto; and my old mate Ashley toured *We Will Rock You*. I have to say, when I first made the move, those girls really made living in London bearable.

What I soon realized was that I'd actually made loads of friends from the show – most of whom lived in London. Before long, I found myself part of a lively social circle. My fabulous friend Alex took me to the Kingly Club to welcome me to the big smoke, and I loved that. The bar was so swanky and stylish; I felt like an A-lister.

I did even more so when John Barrowman invited me to The Ivy one night, along with his partner Scott Gill, Daniel Boys, Ben James Ellis and Ian 'Shirley' Temple. We had the best time, drinking champagne like it was going out of fashion and laughing till we cried.

London really is the place that never sleeps. Even late at night, lying in my bed, I can still hear the hum of traffic from a few streets away. It's amazing.

To make myself feel a little more at home, I modified my pad a touch to make it more Jodie-friendly. Just like my mum, I love to decorate. So, I got my friend Peter to make me these incredible mirrored wardrobes. Bless him, he came all the way down from Liverpool to put them up for me, and now my bedroom looks like a film star's.

Sadly, when I get up in the morning, I don't look like one, and I have to avert my eyes. Nevertheless, it's great. I adore my room – the decor's all black, white and silver with a dash of red.

Being away from home and having to look after myself was harder than I'd anticipated. I had to get my own toilet rolls, for a start, and the pots I put in the kitchen sink didn't magically wash themselves up and put themselves away in the cupboard! Over the past few months, I have gone from being a domestic virgin to a house-proud young woman. Aggie from *How Clean Is Your House?* would be proud of me.

With roughly five months to go before I took on the role of Nancy in the West End, Cameron Mackintosh recommended that I use the time to prepare. In particular, he wanted to make sure that when I walked out on stage for the *Oliver!* previews in December, I was as proficient at acting as I was at singing.

On *I'd Do Anything*, you see, I'd proved that my vocals were strong, but I hadn't yet shown Cameron the best of my dramatic side. I appreciated that I had a lot to learn. Up until then, I'd really only appeared in school and college productions, though I did have some professional acting experience from gigs like *Spooktacular*. I guess you could argue that I definitely used my skills when I was a kid, trying to get out of school. But all that was a long way from playing to audiences who had forked out loads of dosh for a West End seat.

To make them believe I really was Nancy, I needed to be utterly convincing on stage. That meant I would have to knuckle down and study my art. Cameron therefore arranged for me to attend a month-long acting course at the Royal Academy of Dramatic Art (RADA).

On my first day, a sunny morning in mid July, I have to admit I was quite nervous. It was like going back to school again – only this time, I was walking corridors that had once been paced by greats like Sir Anthony Hopkins and Dame Helen Mirren. Oh, and I was pushing thirty. But even though I was older, I still felt like the newbie who didn't know what she was doing.

I'd half expected it to be like *Fame*, with everyone walking along reciting lines from plays or speaking in booming voices. Yet it was just like a normal school, with normal people. In fact, there were a lot of really nice people, who were friendly and not competitive in the slightest, as I'd feared they might be.

As the four-week course commenced, the question that had worked its way into my head wasn't 'To be or not to be?' but 'Can Jodie act or not?' Well, as it turns out, yes, she can. Not only that, but I discovered I had a pretty good left hook, too. Although I was specializing in Shakespeare, we were also taught stage fighting, which I knew would come in handy for my scenes with Bill Sikes in *Oliver!*

The month at RADA truly was great. I made some friends, including Emma Watson, Hermione in the *Harry Potter* films, who was also on the course, although not in my class. Robin Gibbs's son John was a classmate – and yes, folks, I did make a joke about the Bee Gees, I couldn't help myself. You know what I'm like; I have no shame.

The experience wasn't all about the friendships I made. I really came away with something theatrically. I'd never appreciated the works of Shakespeare before; when I was younger, I couldn't understand a word of it. Studying it at twenty-nine, older and very much wiser, I discovered that the language was actually rather beautiful. In fact, I was so excited by the words he had crafted that I thought to myself it was such a shame that Shakespeare wasn't alive any more because he was bloody good at what he did.

It was rather fitting that I was studying the tragedies of Shakespeare, as my time at RADA would give me yet another doomed romance to chalk up to experience, with yet another Mr Not-Quite-Right in a starring role.

The moment I saw him strolling along a corridor, I fell instantly in love. He was tall and handsome and, as I'd later discover, a little older than me, in his forties. It was clear that we both knew there was an immediate attraction. As we shared a lingering glance, he gave me what my mates have since called an 'eye f**k'. I know that sounds crude, but how else do you describe a look like that? I swear, I nearly did a full-on Shakespearean swoon. I was like a bowl full of jelly. I had to rush straight into the nearby disabled toilets, where my knees gave way. Thank God those loos were clean.

At the end of term, Emma Watson invited everyone to a party at Shoreditch House, a trendy members' club in the East

End of London. It was swanky to say the least, with a massive swimming pool on the roof, but it was surprisingly friendly. I liked it there and made the most of the bar. The evening was fab, with loads of fun folks introducing themselves.

But then the night got even better when – emerging from a throng of people – along came the latest object of my desire. After a lot of steely gazes, we eventually mustered up enough courage to speak to each other. And I wasn't let down. You know sometimes you can fancy a guy, but their voice might put you off, or they might be a big dull dud? Well, he was just perfect. He had a deep, manly voice, and when he spoke, he was interesting and funny. Result!

As the night progressed, I knew I was falling for him big time. Oh, Jodie, what are you like? Yes, I'm a sucker for a charmer, I admit. And once again I fell hook, line and sinker. Of course, there was a sting in the tail. It turned out that the gorgeous vision was seeing someone. Yep, seeing someone who wasn't me. I was gutted.

Even though he was apparently happy with his girlfriend, he said he liked me. He even told me, 'You have a face that could destroy Rome.' What a smooth talker, eh? Maybe I should have known better.

It was obvious that things would never work out for us, and they didn't. Along with the problem of his existing girlfriend, I just don't think he could handle my 'media life'.

We met up a few times after the party, though. I felt really bad for his girlfriend, but I couldn't help myself – I was so into him. Every time I saw him was dreamy, until it was time to part, when I knew that he'd be going back to his girlfriend, while I'd trot home to an empty flat; and an empty flat that belonged to Cameron Mackintosh, at that.

In the end, we decided that we had to call it a day. I asked him to meet me for one very last time at the bridge by Embankment station. He never showed. It was the saddest thing ever. I just felt like: how many more times can I put myself out there and get stamped on? We had such a great connection, but it never happened.

Shortly after my course finished, I was invited to perform at the Faenol Festival in Wales on Sunday 24 August. The festival's line-up was impressive, with Boyzone and Cerys Matthews on the bill, but what sold it for me was that, in addition to performing a solo number, I would get the chance to share the stage with my old mate Mr John Barrowman.

For my solo spot, I chose 'Out Here On My Own' from the movie version of *Fame*, but I was much more excited about teaming up with sexy John on the duet 'Come What May', the love theme from the film *Moulin Rouge*.

As I sang my heart out, I was practically shaking with glee. I couldn't believe that I was standing there on that stage, looking into the eyes of this musical legend and hearing our voices soar in harmony. A year ago, I was walking my Yorkshire terriers around Stanley Park in Blackpool – now here I was duetting with John frickin' Barrowman, performing one of the most beautiful ballads ever written.

Halfway through the song, I got swept up in the emotion of the music and lyrics, and for one brief moment I think I may have actually started to fall in love with old John.

'Oh, why does he have to be gay?' I thought. 'I bet he'd treat me better than most of the tossers who have wrecked my life over the years.'

Ah well, Scott, John's even more gorgeous husband, would probably have something to say about that!

At the very end of August, Cameron revealed that he had another fantastic experience up his sleeve for me. It was decided that I should get used to the world of theatre by joining the ensemble of *Les Misérables* at the Queen's Theatre in London.

Despite my excitement about my impending West End debut, I was worried about joining a cast that had already bonded. I had heard so many rumours about 'West End

Wendies', who apparently ponced about all the time, bitching about the actors they reckoned couldn't sing a note. I'd never survive, I was sure of it.

Fortunately, it turned out that I had nothing to fret about in the slightest. Everyone welcomed me with open arms. They were such a great cast to work with and an incredibly talented bunch. They made me feel so at ease when I felt so very nervous.

Even though it was hard work, we always found time to have a good laugh with each other in the dressing rooms. Some nights, when I was playing a beggar, I used to go on stage with my teeth blacked out and that was just hilarious. No, really, it was ... but maybe you had to be there to appreciate just how amusing it was to us in the ensemble.

Climbing the barricade in the show in its infamous battle scene, just like a monkey after a banana, is one of the challenges that ought to go on a list of things to do before you die. It was such an amazing experience. The sense of jubilation is genuine as you scramble up the barricade with the music swirling all around you – even if it did take the wind out of me every night. But one thing's for sure: it kept me trim. Cardiovascular workouts, eat your heart out.

All of the Prengers came down to see me in the musical and I was so proud to be up there performing in front of them. I felt like I had fulfilled their dreams for me. Yet, as it happens, they weren't the only ones to see me strut my stuff. *Les Mis* is such a popular draw that several celebrities, such as Kelly Brook and her rugby star boyfriend Danny Cipriani, came to see the show during my time there.

If you have never seen *Les Mis*, you must. The music is stunning and the story is so tragic, you'll get through a whole box of Kleenex.

Midway through my *Les Mis* run, I was honoured to take part in Andrew Lloyd Webber's birthday celebration in London's Hyde Park on Sunday 14 September: a special concert that was hosted by John Barrowman. I was chuffed to have been included in the line-up, as I got to share the stage with Jason Donovan, Connie Fisher, Ruthie Henshall, Duncan James, Lee Mead, Idina Menzel, Denise Van Outen, Elaine Paige, Joss Stone, and Rhydian from the 2007 series of *The X Factor*, to name just a few.

As I watched awestruck from the wings, these big-name singers belted out one Lloyd Webber tune after another. All I could think was, 'Surely I don't deserve to be here, rubbing shoulders with all these great stars?'

But then it dawned on me that I could be just as good. The atmosphere was electric and I knew that the audience would bring out the best in me. Also, I really wanted to impress the Lord. Slowly, I felt my confidence build, and with that in my heart, I couldn't lose.

I was to sing 'You Must Love Me' from the film version of *Evita*. I'm telling you, stepping out on to that stage in front of tens of thousands of music lovers, I felt just like Britney Spears (almost). As I made my entrance, I was more nervous than I had felt in a long time. This wasn't performing at a gay club in Blackpool. This was a million times different – and a lot more stressful.

Unfortunately, my performance didn't run as smoothly as I'd hoped it would. The cello that was due to accompany me hadn't been plugged in, so while technicians fiddled about behind me, I turned to the thousands of people standing patiently in the park and told them to talk amongst themselves while the problem was sorted out. Luckily, that got a giggle.

Eventually, everything was ready and I began to sing. I don't know how I sounded, but I guess I must have done an okay job because the crowd went wild when I'd finished. The sound of the applause was amazing. This was what I had always wanted: the chance to entertain thousands of people. And there I was, doing it – and alongside the likes of Jason Donovan and Lee Mead. I couldn't contain my excitement.

Also in September, I threw myself into my charity work

and became a patron for the Great Ormond Street Hospital appeal, Theatres for Theatres, which aims to raise £4 million over three years to fund two new operating theatres, which will be employed specifically to treat patients with neurological and craniofacial conditions. As part of the fund-raising drive, I performed at a launch event for the charity. It was such a fabulous evening, with an array of celebrities showing their support.

I have to say on a personal level how wonderful it is to be part of this. I know from my own visits to the hospital how hard all the staff work and what a happy place they create for the kids. The children themselves are adorable – you just want to give them the biggest hugs.

Suddenly, in what felt like no time at all, my run in *Les Mis* came to an end. Even though I was leaving to start rehearsals for *Oliver!*, I was sad. The guys and gals had made me feel so welcome that I almost didn't want to go. But I knew I had to; I had a starring role to perfect.

When I left, the cast gave me a huge framed picture of them all, which they'd all signed. It was stunning. Of course, I burst into tears in the way only Jodie Prenger can. I still miss them all, although I am lucky enough to have kept in touch with many of them.

I learned so much from my very first West End experience, like how pressured it is to work night after night in a show that is technical and involved. More than anything, though, it made me realize that I was doing what I really wanted to do.

And with that realization, I knew that the time had finally arrived for me to assume the role I was destined to play: Nancy, in the West End stage musical *Oliver!* With the first rehearsal just around the corner, I wondered if I could really pull it off. I was about to find out.

27

The Day of Reckoning

On Thursday 30 October 2008, I woke up filled with a mix of nerves and excitement. Finally, the time had arrived. I was about to start work on my first big production, in which I would be one of the leads ... and perform alongside the likes of Rowan Atkinson, Julian Glover and Burn Gorman, no less. This really was the most important day of my life to date. I suddenly realized that, from this moment on, nothing would ever be the same again.

Dramatic, I know, but you have to understand that for years, as I struggled to succeed on the club circuit, I never really thought I'd make it big, and end up with a proper career like this. There were times when I thought that perhaps each of my shows at the clubs would be my last.

I certainly never expected to end up in the West End, performing to thousands of theatregoers who had shelled out around fifty quid on a ticket. My life was about to move up a gear. I knew that I couldn't just bluff my way through this, the way I sometimes had on a few of my disastrous nights at working men's clubs. Now I had to show the world what I was capable of.

Consequently, you can imagine how nervous I was. Today was the day I'd meet the rest of the cast as a whole; when I'd finally have to put my money where my mouth was and prove to them that the public had made the right decision in choosing me for the role.

As I grabbed a quick breakfast and took a shower, I couldn't help but fret over the worst-case scenarios that could take place when I walked into the rehearsal studio. What if I strutted in, tripped up and went arse over tit in front of everyone? Or worse still, what if I couldn't act after all and failed to make the part as convincing as I needed to?

Sure, I had spent the summer doing my acting course at RADA, but that was all theory. Learning the ropes in those hallowed halls, I hadn't been performing in front of a real audience and nerves weren't exactly an issue. Today, I knew that I had to make sure that I impressed Cameron and the rest of the team. I had to ensure that they saw me as a worthy cast mate, and not just someone who had got lucky and won a reality show.

In my heart of hearts, I knew I could do it, but there's always that part of you that thinks you won't cut the mustard. I was genuinely concerned that some of my colleagues might not look favourably on me because I'd landed the job via a TV show. I reckoned some of them might think, 'How dare this northern club singer just stride into our show like this?' But I was determined to show them that I could do anything.

What made me most nervous was the idea of working with Rowan Atkinson, who was taking on the part of Fagin. Yes, the star of *Blackadder*, one of the funniest TV series ever – and Rowan is one of my favourite actors of all time. The idea of working opposite a comedy legend every night (and not just any comedy legend, but one I worship) was hard to process.

Rowan is a big star – and has a reputation of being rather intense. I told myself that he was probably not the kind of man to suffer fools gladly. I feared that he might not have the patience to deal with someone who hadn't had as much theatre experience as him. I knew that he didn't do shows like *Oliver!* that often, so this was a big deal. The last thing

I wanted to do was to let him down, and make a show of myself in the process.

I had actually met Rowan a few weeks before, when the principal cast members had gathered together to do promo shots, which would be used to publicize the production. Although I'd become used to having my picture taken since winning *I'd Do Anything*, it was daunting to be sharing the frame with such an esteemed actor as Rowan. I was immediately in awe of him. I mean, I wasn't left speechless or anything – can you imagine me short of a word or two? Didn't think so! – but I thought to myself, 'This is the one and only Rowan Atkinson.' Would he really tolerate a newbie like me?

Once I slipped on my Nancy dress, however, I wasn't Jodie Prenger any more. I *was* Nancy, the villainous criminal who kidnaps young Oliver and lives to regret it. We all had so much fun fooling around and getting into character that it didn't feel like we were working. I couldn't believe I was being paid to do it.

As I headed off to my first ever rehearsal at the 3 Mills Studios in Bromley that October morning, my tummy was full of butterflies. Nerves and doubts swam around my head like piranhas, eagerly nipping away at what confidence I had left. When my cab pulled up at the old mill studio buildings, I knew the moment had arrived. There was no going back now.

(Well, there was. I could have quite easily turned on my heel and headed straight back to my flat, packed up my gear and fled back to Blackpool, but we all know that isn't me. I'm a fighter, and I was keen to make my mark.)

As I pushed open the doors of the rehearsal room, the sound of the kids' singing engulfed me. They burst into a wonderful rendition of 'Consider Yourself' as I stepped into the room ... and it was all for little old me. They were performing it for me as a welcome to the cast, which was so moving. I fell in love with the young 'uns there and then. I mean: how amazing is that? I felt like I was in a scene from a film.

With that warm welcome, I suddenly felt at home, despite the daunting rehearsal that lay ahead. Sure, the pressure was still there, but a sudden wash of excitement swept over me and immediately reminded me what it was I was there to do.

Cameron greeted me with a big hug. Then he introduced me to Rupert Goold, the director. At this stage of proceedings, I wasn't sure what to make of him. From what I'd seen on the telly or in films, I was expecting the director to be a shouty guy, who barked orders at anyone who put a foot wrong or forgot a line. I was pleasantly surprised to find that Rupert is a calm and lovely man. As I would later discover, Rupert is a very supportive director. He was laid-back and patient throughout, and has a gift for bringing out the best in people.

As we chatted, I could sense my new cast mates looking at me, no doubt giving me the once-over before they ventured across to say hi. I wondered if they would be as welcoming as the *Les Mis* cast; they had taken me under their wing so quickly, and I could only hope that this new set of people would be just as friendly.

Of course, this cast had a few more well-known faces, which made me feel a bit more tense. Aside from Rowan, whom I noticed was sitting rather quietly across the hall, there was Burn Gorman, set to play Nancy's lover Bill Sikes, whom I recognized from TV shows like *Torchwood*. He strode over and greeted me with a firm handshake and a hug. I was immediately at ease with him; he's such a down-to-earth fella.

Rowan was a treat to meet again. He strolled up, extended a hand and announced, 'I'm Rowan Atkinson.' As if I didn't already know. Come on, everyone's spent the past few decades in stitches watching this guy perform. Yet I loved the fact that this massive star was such a lovely, normal guy.

Oddly, despite the fact that he was so polite, I still felt intimidated by him. I had no reason to be. He may be a huge celebrity, but he certainly doesn't act that way. He is the most humble, modest man I have ever met.

Yet although Rowan made it easy to be with him, I couldn't help but think back to the days when I'd been in awe of him in *Blackadder*, and feel unworthy. Growing up, I loved the show and thought Rowan was a genius. Now here I was, not only sharing oxygen with him, but also starring opposite him in this blockbuster of a West End production.

Once the introductions were out of the way, it was straight down to work for our first read-through. We were all given the script and, sitting around a table, ran through it as a group to get a feel for the show. Even though we were basically just saying our lines aloud, I still felt petrified with nerves.

As the story unfolded, I looked about me at the fabulous actors sitting beside me. This wasn't like a school play or am dram: this was for real. I was hearing the rich voices of stars of the Royal Shakespeare Company and Hollywood – performers who had years of experience to draw on when shaping their characters, while I had very limited acting experience.

When it came to speaking my first line, I was convinced that I would fluff it up … but I didn't. All right, so I might have rushed it a bit, but once I got into my stride, I could feel my panic subside and I began to relax. In fact, I actually started to enjoy myself.

Frustratingly, there were moments when I read the lines aloud and then immediately thought that I should have done them another way. When I spoke to Rupert about it later, he assured me that this had just been our first run-through: there was loads of time for me to find the right voice for Nancy and turn the character into my own.

The experience was nothing like I thought it would be. Playing Nancy on *I'd Do Anything* had been a whole other kettle of fish. This process was a lot more raw. I knew that I had to give Nancy more depth and more feeling than I had when I'd tried to channel her in the TV show. Discovering her true nature and interpreting it on stage would be hard, but I was more than up for the challenge.

From then on, rehearsals followed a structure of reading through a variety of scenes each day. We also worked on the songs and tackled the routines and choreography. It was tough, especially learning the blocking – the physical staging of the scenes, such as where I stood to say a certain line, or when I moved to the left. There was a lot to remember, and that scared me.

To start with, it all seemed too much. I would take ages to get the words in my head or work out in which direction I should be walking mid scene. But then, as the days passed, I gradually found it easier to sing, act, dance and think at the same time. I know I make it sound like it was as complex as brain surgery, but when you're contemplating so many things simultaneously, it is hard to work it all out. As I soon discovered, though, once you get lost in the production, combining all those skills becomes second nature.

Of course, I wasn't the only amateur taking part in the show. The three winning Olivers who had appeared on *I'd Do Anything* were just as new to it as I was. There was eleven-year-old Laurence Jeffcoate from Cheshire, with whom I'd sung 'Getting To Know You' during the final; twelve-year-old Harry Stott from Oxfordshire, who is adorable and a fab little actor; and eleven-year-old Gwion Wyn Jones from Carmarthenshire, who is just cute and tiny. I really can't pick between them as to my favourite: all of them are so talented.

I have to say I was very proud of them. I mean, it was tough enough for me, a grown-up, to deal with all of this, but they were like proper little adults, taking everything in their stride. If they were nervous, they never showed it. They were troupers, taking to the acting lark like ducks to water. When they read their lines and did run-throughs, they were professional and looked as if they'd been in showbiz for thirty years.

Maybe they weren't kids after all. Maybe they were tiny little midgets trying to pull the wool over my eyes.

There's that saying, 'Never work with animals or children', but I must admit that working with the kids has been one of the best parts of this experience. They're all so adorable that you can't help but develop a mother's love for them. Some of the scenes in the play can be quite scary and aggressive, and I always panic that the children are going to get upset, particularly when Nancy is confronted by Bill Sikes. Whenever I come offstage after those bits, to this day, I always high-five the kids so that they know everything is A-okay.

As we started to block the scenes, we all began to see what we were like in character. Burn Gorman really surprised me, as he was absolutely petrifying as Bill Sikes. When he was 'in the zone', he was truly scary, twisting and contorting his face, a million miles from the warm-hearted family man he is in real life. It was an amazing transformation – the sign of a great actor. One minute, he'd be prowling the stage like a madman, and the next he'd be cracking jokes and fretting about how his other half was due to give birth on our opening night and that he might miss it. Talk about bad timing, eh?

Julian Glover, who plays Mr Brownlow, was another absolute gent. After one of our rehearsals, he said to me – and I'll never forget it – 'I can see we are all going to fall in love with Nancy.' What a lovely thing to say: and this from a man who has such a great history in film and theatre. Did you know? He's the only actor to have appeared in the *Star Wars*, James Bond, *Indiana Jones* and *Harry Potter* film franchises.

After a couple of weeks of working on the show in the studios, we moved to the theatre on Drury Lane to continue our rehearsals. I'd been at the venue once before for a mission during *I'd Do Anything*, in which we'd had to train with a stunt artist. Now it was the real thing.

Let me tell you, the minute you walk through the theatre's doors, you get swept up in the majesty of the whole place.

Not only because of its cultural history – many of our greatest ever thespians have at some time acted their hearts out on that very stage, before four tiers of audience – but also because the architecture is so lavish and ornate. Words simply cannot describe how beautiful it is. Because of the stunning surroundings, I found it all rather intimidating. I told myself that in this theatre in particular, there was no room for being slack. You have to give your all out of sheer respect.

With my ghostly past, I was intrigued to learn that the site (which dates all the way back to 1648, if you please) is supposed to be haunted. In fact, it's renowned as one of the most haunted theatres in London, which *is* an achievement. According to the staff, though, I needn't worry about the spirits hurting me in any way. Apparently, if they are seen, it is actually a good-luck sign that the production will have a lengthy life. So 'bring 'em on' is what I say. Besides, I ain't scared of no ghost.

Rehearsals in the theatre were in many ways much more demanding than the studio sessions, and we had one or two mishaps along the way. One afternoon, Burn and I were running through the scene in which Nancy is confronted by the dastardly Bill Sikes at London Bridge. As I went to move away from Burn mid scene, I lost my footing and fell to the ground, smashing my chin as I went.

Two things flashed through my mind as I hit the floor. Firstly: 'Will this mean I'm out of the show?' And secondly: 'Will I end up being the first Nancy to look like Bruce Forsyth or Jimmy Hill?' Luckily, I wasn't hideously disfigured by my accident and managed to continue the rehearsal without further ado.

The days were long and tough, as we struggled to take everything in on an ever-shortening schedule. We had to work out exactly what we were doing on that massive stage and master the technical aspects of the production. It was exhausting, but occasionally, after a full day of sweating and slaving over our roles, we would all enjoy a few beverages out on the town, usually at the local pub Nell's … but never too many because we always had to be up early the next day.

It wasn't all work during this period. Around the time we started rehearsals, I was invited to be in the studio audience for an episode of *Strictly Come Dancing*. I didn't hesitate in going along, taking my mate Jill, the dialect coach on *Oliver!*, with me.

I was so excited as I adore the programme. Ballroom is, after all, in my blood: I grew up in Blackpool, the home of the ballroom-dancing competition. I remember I used to sit for hours watching the contestants who were staying at my parents' hotel, absolutely mesmerized as they sewed beads and jewels on to their dresses. The whole thing looked so glamorous. Give me a posh frock and a few show-stopping moves and I'm as happy as Larry.

The weirdest part of the night for me was that *Strictly* was filmed in the same studio as *I'd Do Anything*, so I had a strong case of déjà vu walking up to the building, only to discover that the studio had been transformed into a fabulous ballroom.

The episode itself was a joy. I loved watching Austin Healey, Tom Chambers, Rachel Stevens and others fly across the floor as they showcased their dancing skills. It was a brilliant spectacle – one that I wouldn't mind trying myself one day, should I get the chance. Jill and I had a blast that evening, and when we watched the show back later, there we were in the front row, clapping away like seals.

In November, just three weeks before our first preview, the cast of *Oliver!* was invited to perform a medley of songs from the show on Children in Need. I felt so privileged to be asked to sing, as I had watched the money-raising telethon for years and knew that it attracted many wonderful stars, such as Kylie and Madonna, who were willing to help the worthy cause.

The ensemble was to sing 'Food, Glorious Food', 'Where Is Love?', 'Consider Yourself' and 'I'd Do Anything'. Even though the staging was a rather potted version of the full musical, we prepared as though it was our opening night and were consequently addled with nerves before we went out on stage.

First up were the kids, who opened with 'Food, Glorious Food'. I looked on from the wings with pride. They were amazing; I was thrilled that all the rehearsals had paid off. When I came out for my spot, my heart was beating hard. This was the first time we were performing as an ensemble for a real audience, so it was a huge deal. In addition, they showed a clip of me winning *I'd Do Anything*, so once again those exhilarating feelings of jubilation came flooding back.

The medley went down a storm. It was wonderful to be able to show the audience a sneak preview of what we'd been working so hard on, and they seemed to relish it. 'I'd Do Anything' is a song in which Nancy interacts with all the kids and shows her warm, caring side, and I felt that I brought that to the fore with my bubbly, 'mother hen' interpretation. The whole thing whetted my appetite for the genuine curtain-up in just a few weeks' time.

After our performance, the mighty Terry Wogan chatted with us. Now, normally, the act of meeting this living legend would have made me a gibbering wreck, but because I had already spoken to Terry on the phone the day before, I was really rather relaxed about it all.

His call had come as I was being driven to the BBC for rehearsals. He interviewed me on Radio 2 to plug a prize that Cameron Mackintosh had kindly donated to Children in Need: four box tickets for *Oliver!*, plus champers, a slap-up meal and the chance to have a backstage tour with yours truly. Listeners were invited to call in with pledges and in the end £20,000 was raised, which was fantastic.

I have to say, speaking to Terry on the phone was one of

those moments I'll cherish till the end of my days. He is so funny. I was chatting away to him like he was an old friend. When I met him in person the next night, he was such a gent.

It's funny when you stop to think about it: the year before, I'd watched Children in Need from my sofa in Blackpool; now, I was running around backstage. Since appearing on *I'd Do Anything*, I had done so much. I'd not had a moment to sit down and think about what I'd achieved. That night, as celebs dashed to and fro around me, I realized that I was living a very privileged life.

Naturally, hard work came with it. The long days continued throughout November and into December, with the whole *Oliver!* team's energies focused on one collective aim: to ensure that, when the show finally opened on 14 January 2009, it would be perfect.

Yet before we could fully concentrate on that opening night – when critics would no doubt be sharpening their knives to find something wrong with my performance (or so I feared) – we had to worry about the previews, which were due to start on Friday 12 December 2008.

Every West End production has previews: a (in our case, month-long) run of performances before a new show officially opens, to which the public are invited but not the press; they're essentially practice runs of the show to flush out potential problems with set, staging, and so on, and to give the cast and crew time to correct any flaws before the proper run starts.

As the first preview came closer, the cast's excitement levels went through the roof. When you are rehearsing something like that for so long, you are just desperate for other people to see it. You can't wait. I was having sleepless nights … not because I was worried about screwing up, but because I couldn't wait to get out there on stage.

Another thing that I was really looking forward to was our first full dress rehearsal. I'd tried on my Nancy dress for the promo shots, but I hadn't had a chance to do any proper acting in it yet. The costume felt so different from the brightly coloured frock I'd worn on *I'd Do Anything*. I felt that once I put that gritty dress on, it would be even easier for me to channel Nancy.

As Friday 12 December approached, I felt giddy. Finally, we'd be performing in front of a live audience, who would react to our every move, gag and note, *and* we'd all be in costume. Hoorah!

Mum, Dad and Marko – bless them – all headed down to London to support me. They were so excited, giving me big hugs and telling me that they knew I'd be brilliant. Yet before I could slip into my Nancy outfit, Cameron announced that he was postponing the first two previews.

At first, I thought his decision had something to do with me. Well, you always think the worst, don't you? But it turned out that he wanted to rearrange a few scenes, which involved a lot of work because of the technical aspects of the production and the large cast. Very fairly, he said that as people were paying to see the shows, he wanted to make sure that they were worth the money. I understood what he was saying – but all that excitement that had been building up was suddenly popped like a balloon.

At least the postponement gave me the chance to hang out with my family. It had been a while since they'd seen me. My mum was particularly impressed by how domesticated I had become. The flat was almost spotless and she could see that I was cooking for myself. Of course, the minute my mum was there, it was all too tempting to have her at my beck and call …

The next morning, 13 December, I woke up early and was petrified; more nervous than I had been the day before, in fact. Yet I didn't mind, because I knew that the nerves would help me to give a great performance – or so I hoped. By 9 a.m., I was at the theatre, working through scenes with

Rupert and the cast. There was no rest for the wicked. We needed to make sure everything was running smoothly for this most significant of days.

In the afternoon, we had a dress rehearsal for an invited audience of around 500 people, including our nearest and dearest, and the show's producers. When I made my entrance, I was able to see my mum, dad and brother staring up at me – along with Ashley Russell, my old mate from *I'd Do Anything*.

While I'd thought beforehand that seeing them might put me off, their presence actually gave me the security to shine even more. The show went swimmingly well: so much so that when we took our final bow, we were given a standing ovation. The applause sounded thunderous in that vast auditorium.

After the dress run, my family and I headed for a quick dinner. Sadly, I couldn't kick back and relax because I soon had to head back to the theatre for the very first public show.

Having enjoyed such a great afternoon, I was full of confidence about the upcoming preview. In some ways, it felt like I glided through it. It was exhilarating to be up there on stage, hearing the crowd reacting to my performance. It was truly electrifying. Knowing that there were 2,300 people out there, all swept up in the story we were telling, was enough to fill me with such a buzz that I forgot I was Jodie Prenger. For that two-hour block, I was Nancy. I felt like I was living and breathing her.

As I'd suspected, the costume helped too. My hair was scraped back, my make-up was coarse and my dress was tattered and dirty. I could practically feel Nancy's spirit ooze into me.

After the lights dimmed on the final scene, we took to the stage for our curtain call. When I danced out to take my final bow, the audience went wild. My eyes filled with tears. I couldn't believe the reaction. It appeared that they liked me, and that's all I could ever have asked for. These were the people who had put me where I was: without their votes, I wouldn't have won the chance to star in this incredible show. To hear them sound so appreciative meant that I hadn't let them down. My eyes glazed, I bowed and bowed again as the applause rang in my ears.

Once the curtain fell for the final time, all the emotion spilled out of me and I wept like a baby. All my dreams had come true.

After the show, I went to meet the fans who were waiting at the stage door. I was shocked by how many people had come to say hello and ask for autographs. What stunned me more was that some of them had come from as far afield as Manchester, Scotland, even America, all with the intention of seeing me perform.

A couple of little children were also waiting for me, weeping. Their parents told me that having seen me suffer at the hands of Bill Sikes in the show, the kids were distraught and wanted to make sure that I was OK. Bless the little poppets. On a positive note, at least it meant those scenes must have been convincing ...

The whole experience was fantastic. I realized that I had made a mark on the public. They had supported me during *I'd Do Anything* – and here they were again, giving me all the love I needed.

It was such a boost to me, and one that I really appreciated. Especially as my most daunting challenge – *Oliver!*'s opening night, in which I would perform in front of all the top theatre critics – was now mere weeks away. Would I impress them? Could I prove to the world that I really was the perfect Nancy?

Only time would tell.

28

Jodie Prenger is ... Nancy

And now, the end is near ... Yes, the final chapter has arrived. How exciting, because it means that we've reached the bit I've been waiting for – my debut on the West End stage as a leading lady. But we're going to have to hold tight just a little bit longer before we get to the opening night.

Christmas 2008 was spent with Mum, Dad, Marko and all the animals *chez* Prenger. It was odd coming home after the year I'd had. Though it didn't exactly feel different to the norm, I knew I had changed. As 2008 reached its conclusion, I realized that my life was never going to be the same again.

Although I had spent much of my career striving for success and trying new ways to achieve my potential, it had never seemed to work out. Looking back, I guess everything I did gave me the foundation for what I would end up doing. I'm the kind of person who believes in fate, and that things happen for a reason. While some of my previous experiences hadn't turned out in my favour – *The X Factor* or that modelling show, for instance – I had certainly learned a lot along the way. I dare say that if I hadn't had those adventures, I might never have been ready, or found myself in the right mindset, even to think about entering something like *I'd Do Anything*.

I had such a gorgeous Christmas at home. Bless my dad and brother: they drove all the way from Blackpool to pick me up after my performance in *Oliver!* on Christmas Eve, and then brought me all the way back to London again for my show on Boxing Day.

It's always good to be home for 25 December, and this year the four of us – including our mass of pets, of course – had such a lovely family Christmas: we sat down to dinner just as we have always done, and then flaked out on the couch in front of the TV. It was just what the doctor ordered. I relished my time back home because I hadn't had a moment to myself over the past few weeks. I had given my all to the rehearsals and previews, so I'd barely had a second when I could simply be the old Jodie Prenger.

Not that I was complaining, of course. I was chuffed that I was doing well. After all, this was what I had always dreamed of – but there were times when I just wanted to be with my family so that we could talk about the little things, like what they had done that day or who they might have bumped into on the street. Although I was always in touch with them by phone, it wasn't the same as being in Blackpool, getting pampered by my parents. At Christmas, that's exactly what Jodie needed and exactly what she got!

I didn't get the opportunity to enjoy too much relaxation at home, though, because I had to be back in London for more previews. I'd also been invited to appear on the BBC's New Year's Eve extravaganza, which was hosted by Nick Knowles. You know what, ladies? He's a bit of all right, he is – but married.

The show was filmed live from *HMS Belfast* on the River Thames, which was very special. The other guests included Olympic gold medallists, such as Rebecca Adlington, and Alesha Dixon, who was singing her heart out and looking flaming amazing. And then there was me – performing Dolly Parton's '9 to 5'. I was thrilled to be in such great company.

Yet it wasn't all glamour – far from it. As you might expect, standing on the deck of a boat on the River Thames just shy of midnight at the end of December was blimmin' freezing. I thought I was going to end up as a frozen fish finger. As always, though, the BBC treated us like royalty and handed out handwarmers by the dozen. I found them a useful device (you should try sticking them in your bra, girls – not only do they keep your knockers warm, but they double up as a set of chicken fillets; bonus, I say).

Everyone on the programme was really up for some fun. I was on cloud nine that I had been invited on to a TV show to welcome in the new year. How could I have possibly refused? Just twelve months before, I had enjoyed a few drinks with some mates – and now here I was joining millions of viewers to say goodbye to the old year.

As that all-important midnight hour approached, the buzz around me grew stronger. Still, all I could think about was what an incredible year it had been. I'd won a reality show and my dream job; worked with the likes of Andrew Lloyd Webber and Cameron Mackintosh; met one of my idols, Liza Minnelli; and performed in front of thousands of people at Andrew Lloyd Webber's sixtieth birthday celebrations. Not only that, I'd appeared in the West End production of *Les Mis*, and on Children in Need with the cast of *Oliver!* Reviewing the situation (ha!), even I felt impressed by my achievements. In fact, if it hadn't been my life, I think I would have been as jealous as hell.

When Big Ben struck twelve, I wondered what lay in store for me in the coming year. The press night was up first, on 14 January. Although we were in previews, running through the show six times a week, the opening night was the one that we all cared about the most. That was the moment when the production would be up on its feet properly. During the previews, Rupert and Cameron had tweaked aspects of the show: chopping scenes, rewriting the script, restaging some of the routines. From the fourteenth, there would be no more big changes. After that, we'd have jumped off the edge of that cliff and we'd be flying.

But what else would 2009 have up its sleeve? Would there be any room for romance? So far, my luck in love has been bloody awful. You know, I really am beginning to think that all men are from Mars – and if you find a planet further from Venus ... well, that's where I am from. I say that, but nevertheless there is still a die-hard romantic side to me that continues to carry a glimmer of hope, despite everything.

As it was, all thoughts of romance were set aside as the opening night approached. It was now, more than ever, that I realized what a big deal *Oliver!* was. Of course I knew it was a massive production, so I'd anticipated that there would be a lot of interest, but little did I appreciate just how much. According to reports, advance ticket sales were at £15 million, making it the fastest-selling show in theatre history. How amazing is that – especially in the current economic crisis, when shows are closing left, right and centre. Just to be part of that achievement was enough to give me shudders.

While Rowan's involvement was an obvious major pull, I was chuffed to bits when a BBC news report suggested that my win on *I'd Do Anything* had also helped to push up the ticket sales. They reckoned that the series had introduced theatre to a whole new set of people, many of them from the younger generation. If that's the case, it's brilliant. People slag off reality shows so much, but they forget that programmes like *Any Dream Will Do* and *I'd Do Anything* can actually do a lot of good. With TV dominating culture the way it does, youngsters wouldn't normally even consider going to the theatre. They'd just stay at home, playing a video game or watching a DVD. Thanks to these shows, they now have the taste to go and see a musical.

If I have been part of that change in any way, then I am the proudest person alive. That sounds a bit worthy, I know, but I am pleased to think that by appearing on the show, I may have helped to change someone's outlook in some way – because you really can't beat live theatre. There is nothing like it. No two nights are ever the same. Every actor brings something different to each show and you never know what might happen ... or go wrong. You can't get that from a DVD or a film at the pictures.

When the day of the press night finally arrived, nerves began to set in. Well, actually, I wouldn't say they were nerves as such. I was more excited than scared. If I'm truthful, I couldn't wait to get out there and do it.

Sure, there were going to be reviewers in attendance – watching my every move, perhaps even slagging me off – but I loved performing and I loved the show, and I didn't care what any of those critics made of my performance. All I cared about was what Cameron and Rupert and the other cast members thought. I didn't want to let any of them down. I knew I had the least experience of them all, so I was determined not to be the weakest link. Fortunately, I was never made to feel like I was. I had great support from the whole team, who really seemed to have confidence in me.

Although we naturally fretted about whether we'd remember our lines or hit a bum note on opening night, the thing that was playing on everybody's mind was that Burn Gorman's wife Sarah was due to have her baby on the very same day. Talk about coincidence. Not wanting to miss her hubby doing his thing, she was going to attend that night. We could only hope that some bright spark in the box office would seat her at the end of a row, just in case our rendition of 'Oom-Pah-Pah' induced labour.

I was amazed by how focused Burn was. Of course his mind was elsewhere from time to time – the impending birth of his baby was no doubt the most important thing in his life – but admirably he decided to go ahead with the show and seemed totally intent on making it the best yet.

In the hours leading up to the big night, the theatre was

a sea of activity. TV crews were scattered about, filming reports during our last-minute rehearsals. We were so busy running through scenes or speaking to the press that we barely had a moment to consider the upcoming performance – which was good, because if I'd spent the whole day sat on my own thinking about it, I probably would have dreamed up a million ways I could screw up.

When I finally headed to my dressing room, I stared at myself in the mirror. This was it: my big day. My table was covered with good-luck cards and behind me flowers were strewn about the place, making my room look like a greenhouse. Thank God I don't suffer from hay fever is all I can say – the amount of pollen would have put me in A & E. I was so touched that so many people had sent me good wishes.

The *I'd Do Anything* team excelled themselves with their presents, I have to say. Denise gave me cupcakes, John sent the best champagne, Graham arranged for a stunning display of purple orchids, and Andrew presented me with a decanter engraved with '*Oliver!*'. Their words of support had me in tears – especially the beautiful message in Cameron's card, which reassured me that he approved of my casting 100 per cent.

One of Cameron's gifts was a page from the original programme of the 1905 production of the play *Oliver Twist*. I truly love it: it was the best present I could have been given.

A couple of days before, Cameron had had another surprise for me: one that was better than any material gift in the world. He came by my dressing room to tell me that Lionel Bart's secretary had been to see one of the shows. Afterwards, she had sent Cameron a letter to say that she never thought she'd see someone embody the role of Nancy as well as Georgia Brown, who played Nancy in the original production, had done – but that I had played it just as brilliantly. To hear that from the secretary of the man who had created this unbelievable show was the best compliment I could have imagined.

All afternoon, cast members and stagehands popped in to tell me to break a leg. I was so pleased that everyone got on so well. I went to see Harry Stott, who was playing Oliver that night, to wish him all the best – not that he needed it. He, like the other Olivers, is a very talented boy with a fabulous future ahead of him. Surprisingly, he wasn't that nervous about the impending show. We gave each other a hug and I went back to my dressing room. Later, when the cast was given its thirty-minute call, I started putting my make-up on. The time was nearly upon us.

I discovered that the house was full. Major stars like Terry Wogan, Denise Van Outen, Alan Titchmarsh, Richard Curtis, Tamsin Outhwaite and Barbara Windsor were among the expectant crowd. I had to pinch myself to believe that this was happening. All these famous names and faces were here, and they were about to see me perform. You couldn't make this up.

When the show began, I snuck out of my room to watch the opening scene, in which our fifty or so young 'uns launch into 'Food, Glorious Food'. The kids pulled it off brilliantly. I was so proud that I had tears in my eyes. When the song ended, the audience's applause was deafening. The atmosphere was electric, it really was. I can't quite describe it, but my heart felt like it was skipping because of the energy. It's a cliché, but it's true.

Eventually, three-quarters of the way through the first act, it was time for my debut. I wasn't nervous. I just wanted to get out there and join in the fun. I knew there would be a warm welcome because the show seemed to be going swimmingly. The songs had gone down a treat, while Rowan was ably demonstrating his genius, giving the audience a wittier Fagin than they might have seen before.

When my cue arrived, I stepped in front of the full house. Walking out on stage for the first time, I felt genuine love from the crowd. I soon lost myself in the scene as I clambered down into Fagin's sewer and burst into a rowdy version of 'It's A Fine Life'. In all honesty, the scene flew by faster than I would have liked. I had really wanted to hold on to the experience forever. Instead, I find it hard now to remember exactly what happened, as it was all such a blur. But I got through the song and what I do recall clearly is the end, when the sound of the audience's generous applause was almost enough to knock me off my feet.

Yet that was nothing compared to the reaction I received when I sang Nancy's signature tune, 'As Long As He Needs Me'. I really gave it my all, knowing that this was my moment, my time to shine. As I performed the song, I thought about all the men that I'd once thought I needed. I sang from my soul.

When the key change came, my heart burst with joy: the crowd exploded into applause as my voice scaled the notes, just as I'd hoped they would. I had done it. I had convinced them that I was Nancy. Life couldn't get any better.

As the show careered on, the eager audience gave their seal of approval at every opportunity, laughing and clapping in all the right places. I felt so at home on the stage. This immediate response from the crowd was so infectious and encouraging that you just couldn't help but up your game and give them more and more and more.

That's why theatre is so much more exciting than TV or film. Your performance changes depending on the reactions you receive from the people watching. The audience can draw something out of you that might not have been there if you were filming in front of a small crew and a camera.

When my last scene of the night arrived, my heart sank. I could quite happily have stayed on stage all night. But at least this scene was a dramatic one – one that had had preview audiences in tears and shock. What better way to bow out of a show?

Once I was offstage, tears welled in my eyes. That was me done. My opening-night performance was over. Yet there was one last exciting moment to come: the curtain call. It was, quite simply, amazing. The sound of the audience's applause as the cast trickled back on to the stage was thunderous. It was clear that the show had been a success – as if it could have been anything else under the watchful gaze of the mighty Cameron and his crew.

When I stepped out for my solo bow, the cheers were so immense, I just wanted to burst into tears. All the hard work had paid off. I hadn't let anyone down. I hadn't let Cameron down, or the thousands of people who had put me on that hallowed stage. I was chuffed with myself, I really was. I was so pleased that I had made my friends, cast mates and family proud.

It really is a sight to see a whole audience rise to their feet and clap and clap and clap. Especially when those giving you a standing ovation include people like Andrew Lloyd Webber, Denise Van Outen and Graham Norton – and Suzie, Kate and Martin from the BBC, the producers of *I'd Do Anything*: the people who had started it all. Who cared what the critics had to say when this was the response we'd received?

As the crowd continued to show their appreciation, a huge photograph of Lionel Bart was lowered above the stage and the rapturous applause turned into a roar. I had never met the man myself – he had died years before – but I knew I had a lot to thank him for. Without his gorgeous songs, I wouldn't be there. I looked at the picture and wished I'd known him just a little bit, so that I could have thanked him in person. I'd like to think that wherever Lionel is now, he heard my gratitude as clear as day all the same.

Backstage, Mum, Dad, Marko, our family friends Dave, Carolyn and Stephen, my agent Gav and his other half, and some more pals gathered in my dressing room. Cracking open a bottle of champagne, we toasted the night. I had done it. That all-important first proper performance was over. There was no going back. And in a few short hours, we'd hear what those dastardly critics had to say.

The audience reaction had been enough for me to know that we had pulled off a great show. Yet I also wanted the critics, as unimportant as they were to me personally, to appreciate the hard work we'd put in to make the production succeed.

But before I could think about that, there was a party to attend. At the Waldolf Hilton, no less. Talk about swanky, eh?

Slipping out of my scarlet Nancy dress into a jet-black gown, I felt like a Hollywood star as I fastened jewels around my neck and in my earlobes. A very kind company called Boodles had loaned me a bona fide diamond pendant with matching earrings for my big night, and as the gems glittered in the dressing-room lights, I realized I was a very lucky lady indeed.

I then headed from the theatre to the car, stopping to sign a few autographs along the way. The reaction from the fans was incredible. They seemed so pleased to see me. And even though my agent was keen to move me on so that we could get to the party before it ended, I was quite happy to pose for snaps with fans and sign pictures. After all, these were the very people who had put me where I was. I sure as hell didn't want to be seen as some kind of diva.

The after-show shindig was fabulous, although very busy. I barely got to see my family. In fact, I could hardly walk two feet without someone stopping me and telling me how much they had enjoyed the show, which of course I loved to hear. Really, though, I just wanted to be with my folks. Mum told me that she had never felt so proud of me as she did that night. Screw the critics: it was my mum's opinion that mattered the most.

I'm not sure how long I stayed at the do; it was all a bit of a whirl to be honest. I remember chatting to Babs Windsor and Terry Wogan; and Burn's pregnant wife Sarah, who had, fortunately, not given birth during the performance. She was lovely – although I wasn't sure whether to shake her hand or stroke her bump! I also met Lionel Bart's family. My one big regret is that I never got to meet Lionel himself. Nonetheless, I hoped I had done him proud.

Once I got back to my flat, I chewed the fat with my family and then headed to bed, already intrigued to see what the critics had in store for me the next day. When I awoke, I was not disappointed. Most of the reviews were brilliant – just brilliant – describing the show as a huge success.

My favourite of them all was the one in the *Mirror* by Alun Palmer, which bigged me up good and proper. In fact, I love it so much, I want to recount some of it word for word here, just in case I lose the cutting – not that I will.

'It's a long way from club turns in her native Blackpool,' Palmer wrote, 'but *I'd Do Anything* winner Jodie Prenger took to the West End stage last night and claimed the bright lights of the big city for her own.'

Wow. Good, eh? He went on to say that I looked like 'a veteran of the stage', and concluded with the killer line: 'The night belonged to Jodie.' Well, what could I say to that? I burst into tears. The full review was the most wonderful thing I had ever read. So thank you, Alun, if you are reading this book. It meant the world to me.

But there was more. It turned out that Andrew Lloyd Webber had exited the venue with proud tears in his eyes. I hadn't known that. He was quoted as saying: '[Jodie] really came through [...] She is the people's Nancy.'

The *London Lite* gave the show five stars, while Charles Spencer in *The Telegraph* commented: 'Jodie Prenger brings a warmth to the stage you could warm your hands by, and wrings every last ounce of emotion from [...] 'As Long As He Needs Me'.'

Almost all the reviews brought a smile to my face. Only one was negative. As my mum always told me, though, you're never going to please everybody. I tried my best. Some liked it, some didn't. At the end of the day, I made myself proud – and that's all that counts. I achieved what I used to think was unachievable.

I've come a long way from the Jodie Prenger who was fat in Blackpool. I'm still the same girl at heart; it's just that now I'm half the girl I was, with twice as much going on in my life. If there is a God up there writing the script, I want to say thank you for making my story a fairy tale with a happy ending. (But if you could add in another storyline about me finding a nice normal man, I'd really appreciate that too.)

Oliver! is my life for the next few months. What will happen after that is anyone's guess. All I know is that, at this very moment, I couldn't be any happier. For now, that's really all I can ask for.

Index

(The initials 'JP' denote Jodie Prenger; '*IDA*' denotes the television programme *I'd Do Anything*.)

Index

Index